Dedicated with love to Mom and Marty.

Creating Calm with Butterflies

A Jeanne S Photo Book of Butterflies

by Jeanne Schlesinger

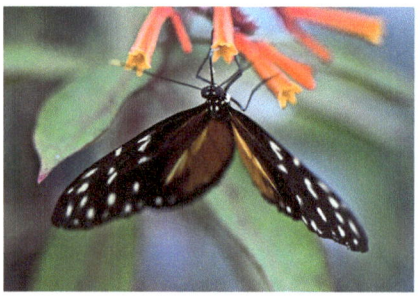

Creating Calm with Butterflies: A Jeanne S Photo Book of Butterflies

©2017 Jeanne Schlesinger

All rights reserved. No part of this book may be reproduced
or transmitted by any form or by any means, electronic
or mechanical, including photocopy, recording,
or any information storage or retrieval system,
without prior written consent from the author.

www.jeannesuniquelens.com

Unique Lens Press
Richmond, VA 23232

Butterflies are magical in so many ways - from their lived lives to the way they symbolize hope, transformation, beauty, and spirit. They are both ancient and modern and are celebrated in cultures all over the world.

Being in their presence feeds my soul. I have been blessed to have access to them for many years at the Butterflies Live exhibit at Lewis Ginter Botanical Garden in Richmond, VA. All of the images in this book were photographed by me and while their actual lives are very short - sometimes just a few weeks - they will live on in these pictures.

I have chosen not to name any of them in writing. Naming things does not come easily to me, but for those of you who are so inclined, I invite you to look on Google, explore in butterfly groups, or in books and delight in having a "scavenger hunt" to see which species are represented in these pictures.

But I also invite you as the viewer to connect with each of these gorgeous creatures visually and celebrate their beauty and uniqueness separate from naming them. This activity is best done when you have a few minutes to be still and quiet and allow yourself to connect with them in a way that excludes words.

Feel your reactions to different images and see which ones speak to you the most. Different butterflies may talk to you in different ways. For example, the white butterfly on page 9 speaks to me as if she is wearing an elegant wedding dress and her white legs look like long gloves. The butterfly at the top of page 5 looks like he is embarking on an epic journey like that of Odysseus. And the butterfly on page 31 disguises herself as a dead leaf on the outside, but when she feels safe enough to open up, she reveals the brilliant colors hiding on the inside. The delight on the young woman's face on page 30 when a butterfly lands on her hand mirrors how I feel every time I have the privilege of being with these amazing creatures.

Engage with these pictures, lose yourself in their beauty, symbolism, and playfulness. Allow their incredible nature to seep into your heart and transform your mood and your energy whenever you feel the stress of the world and are in need of respite.

My hope is that this new way of looking at them will allow their magic to seep into your life in fresh, creative ways. May they invite you to slow down, experience serenity, and revel in the mystery of nature.

In celebration of beauty,

Jeanne Schlesinger

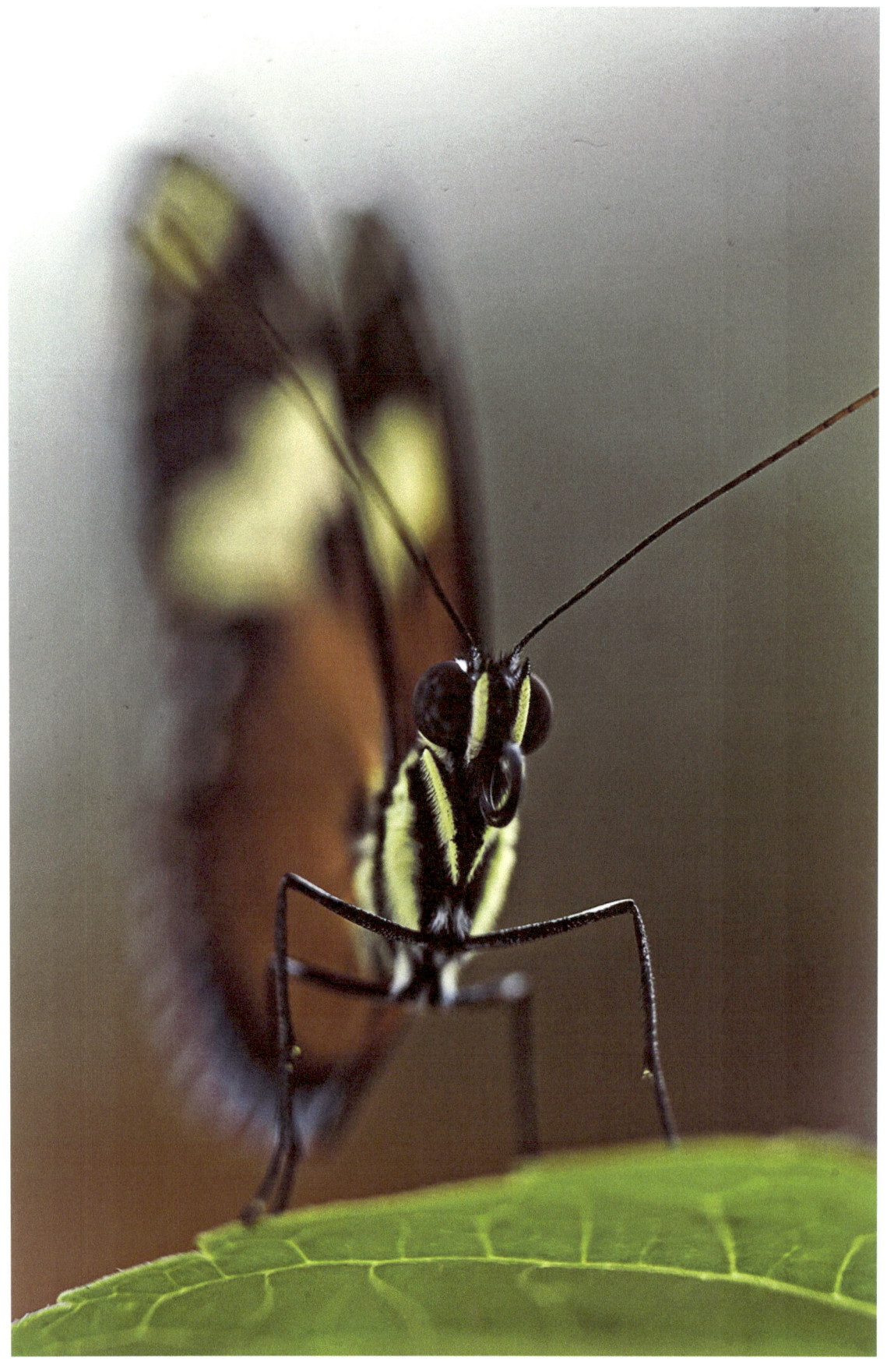

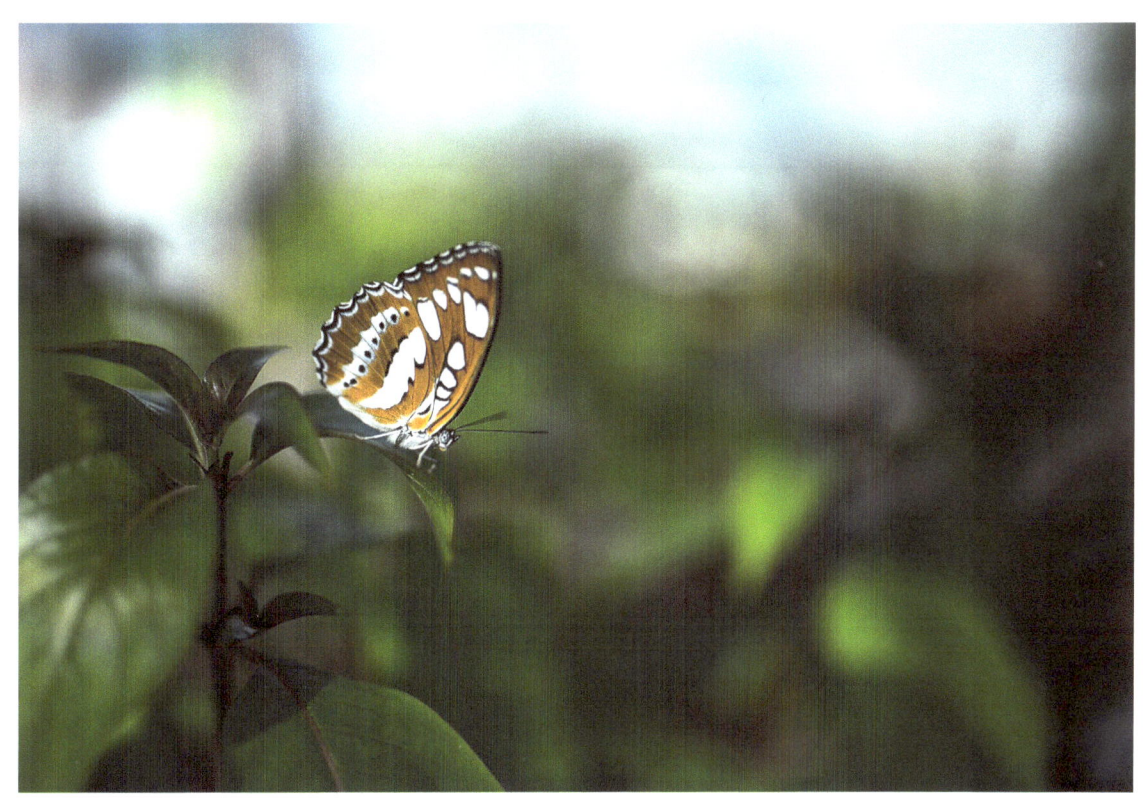

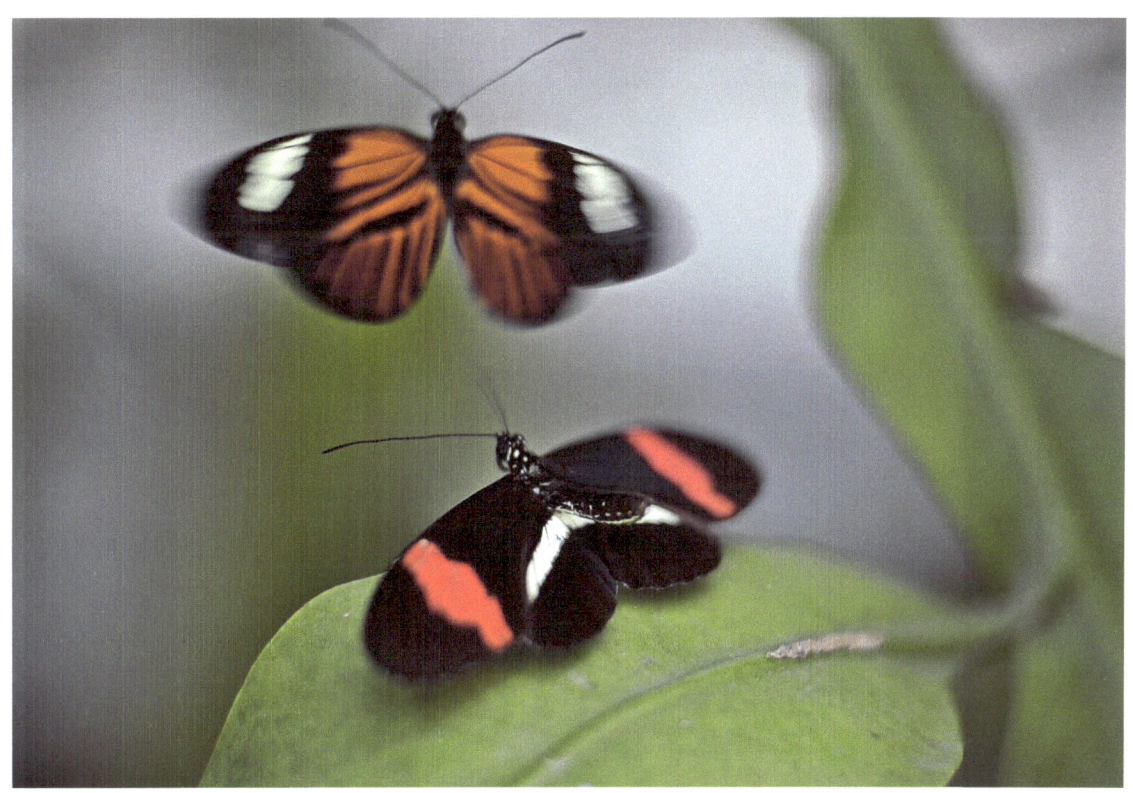

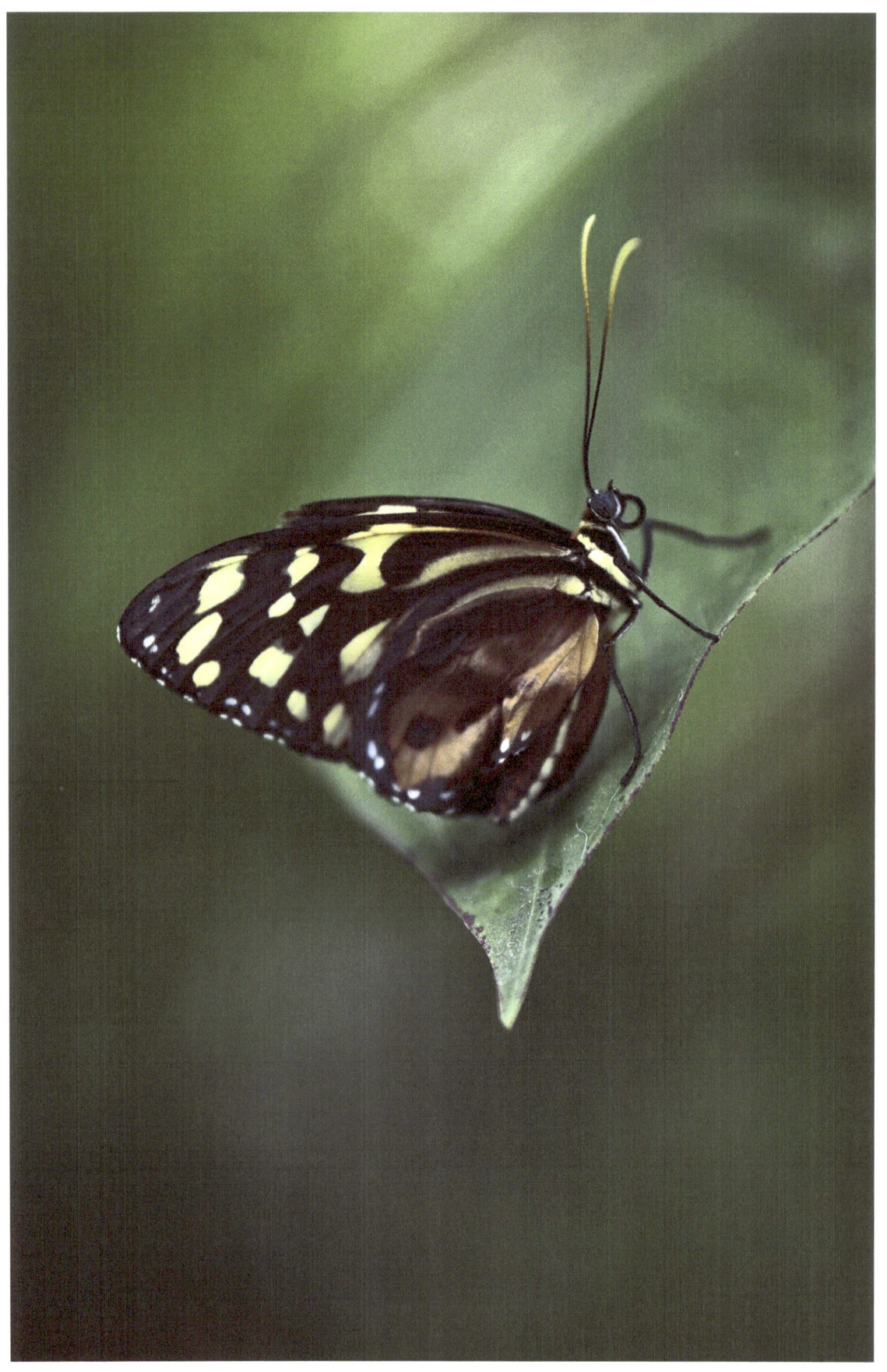

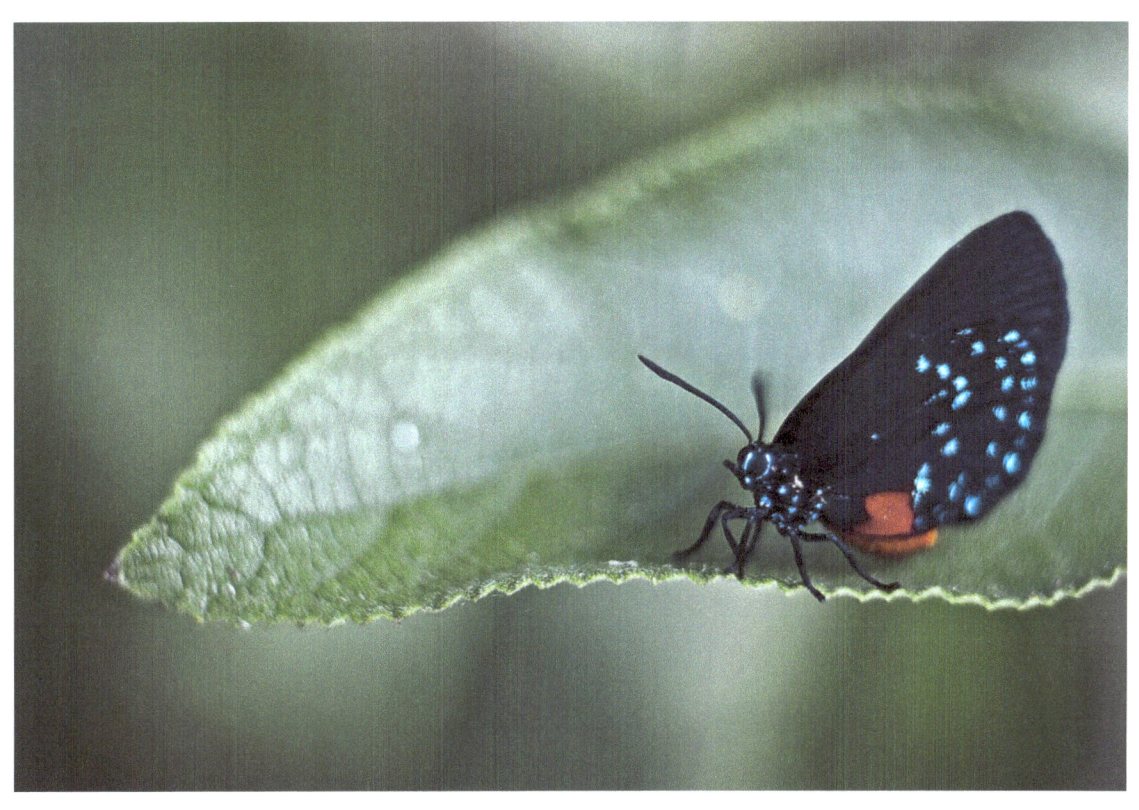

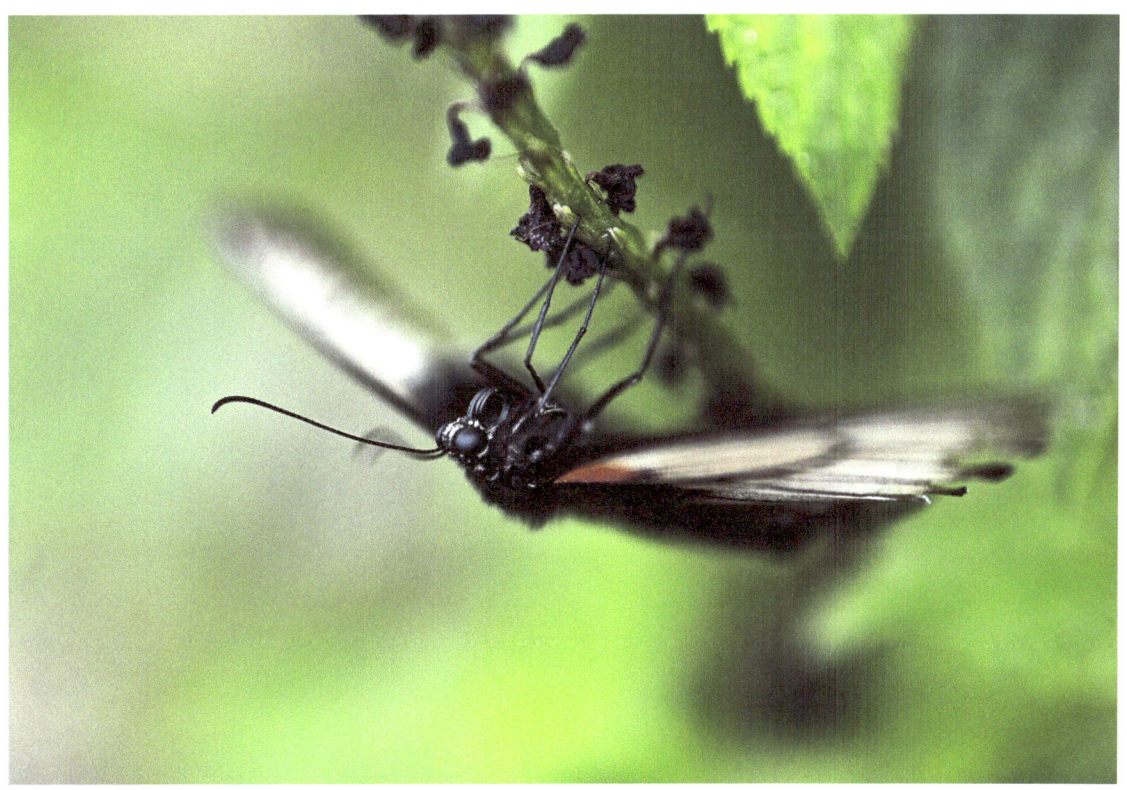

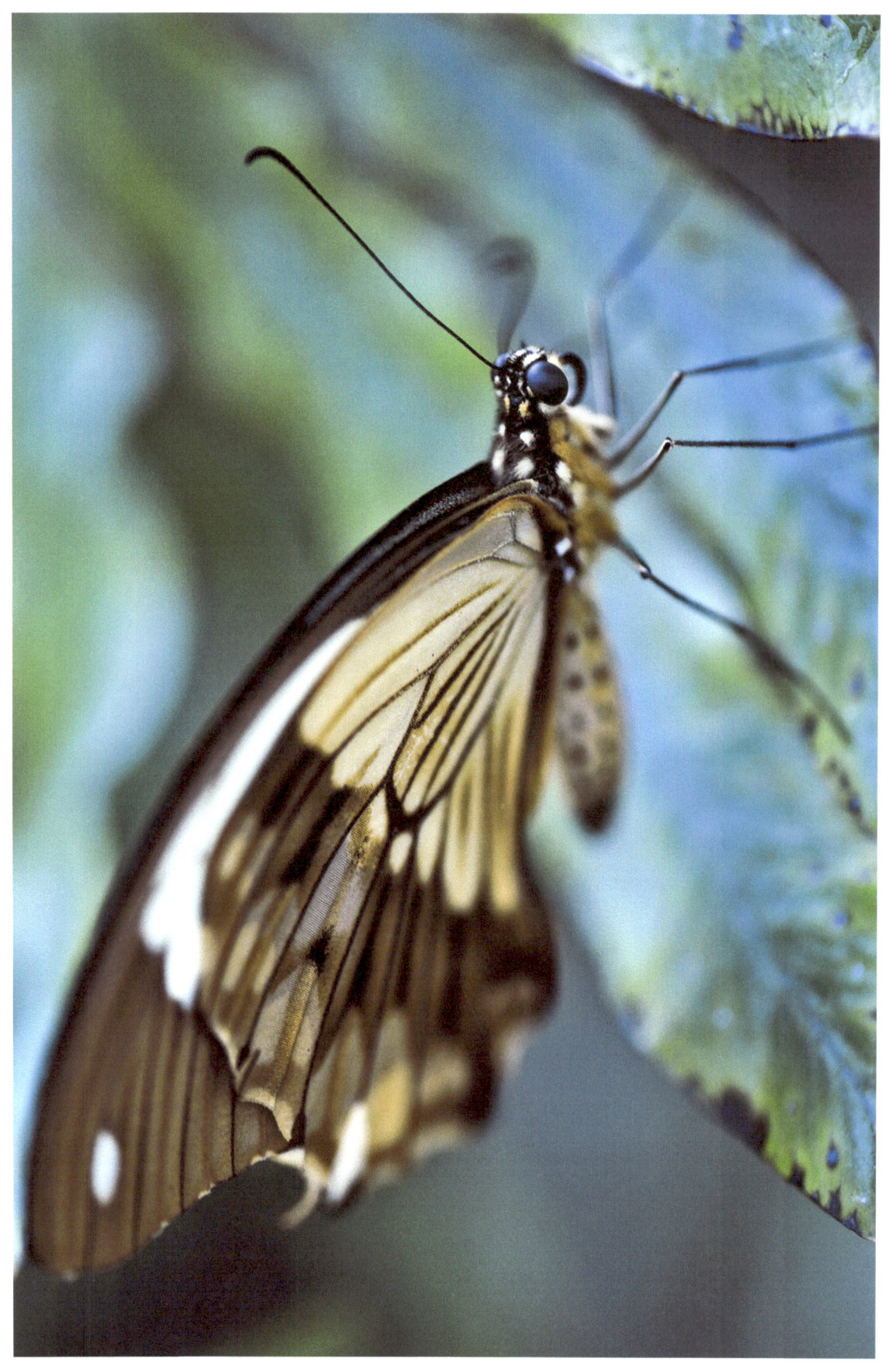

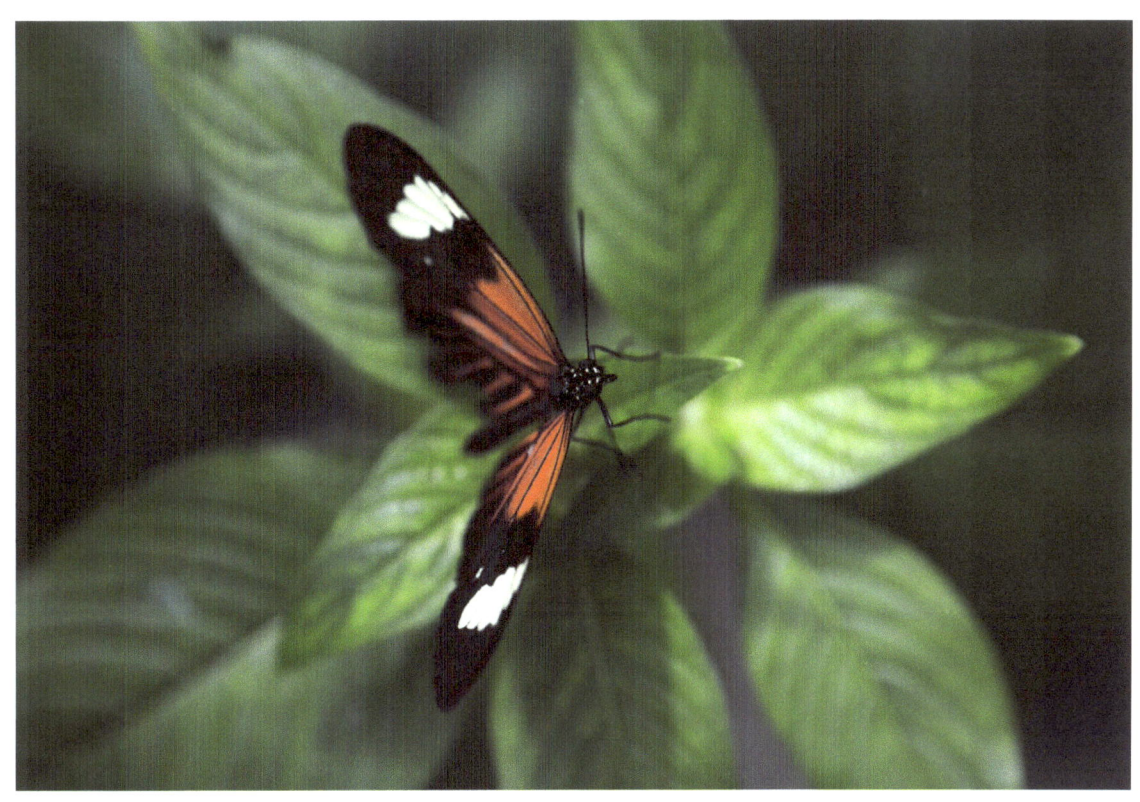

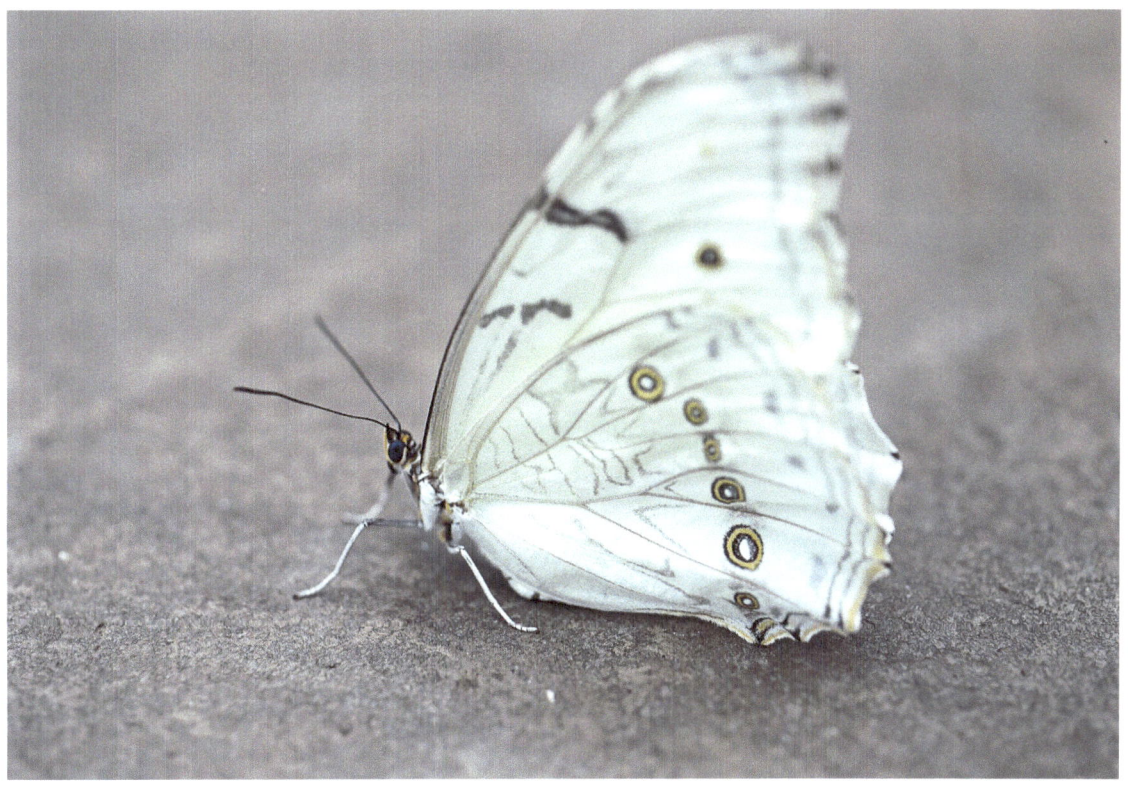

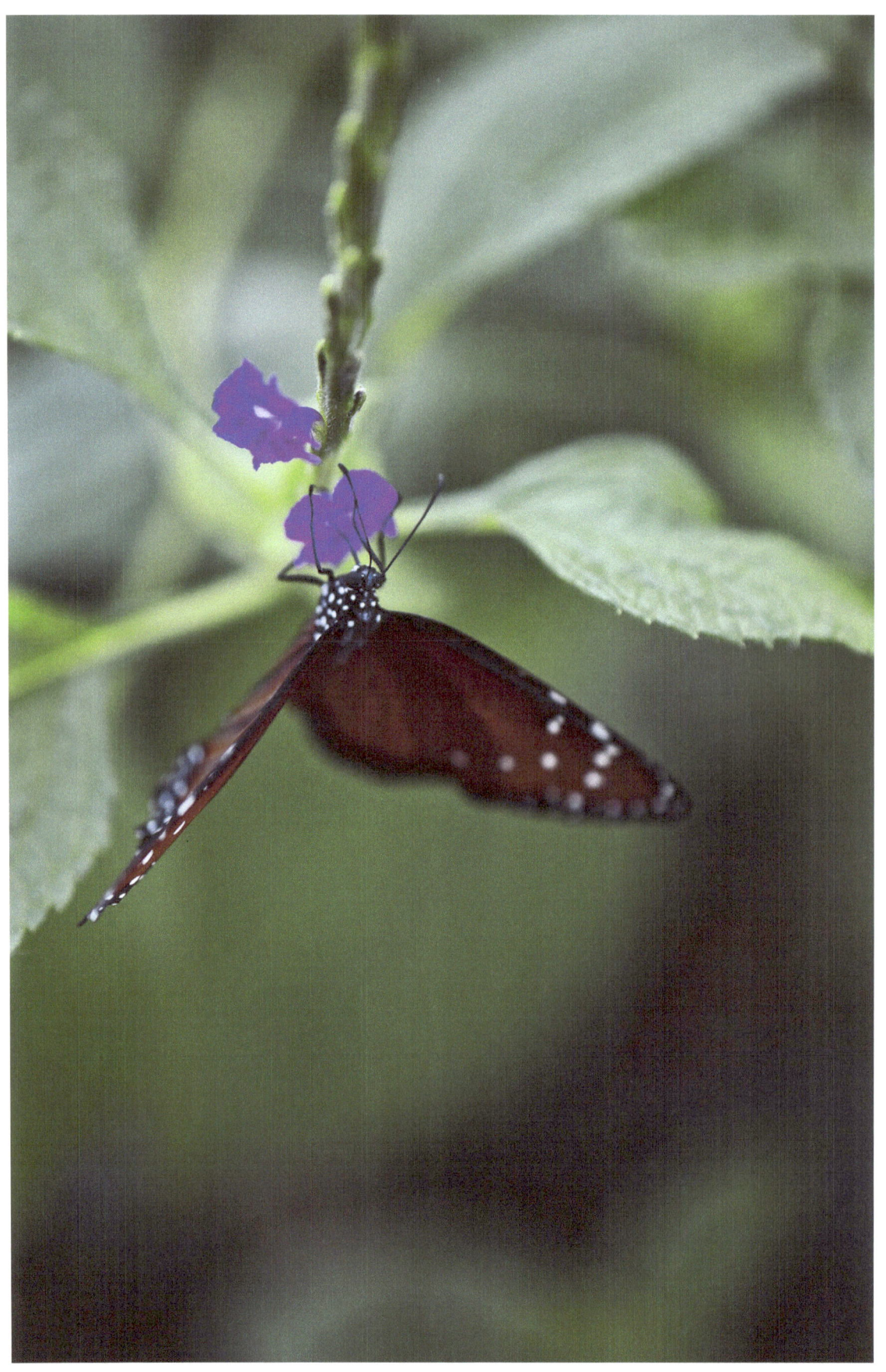

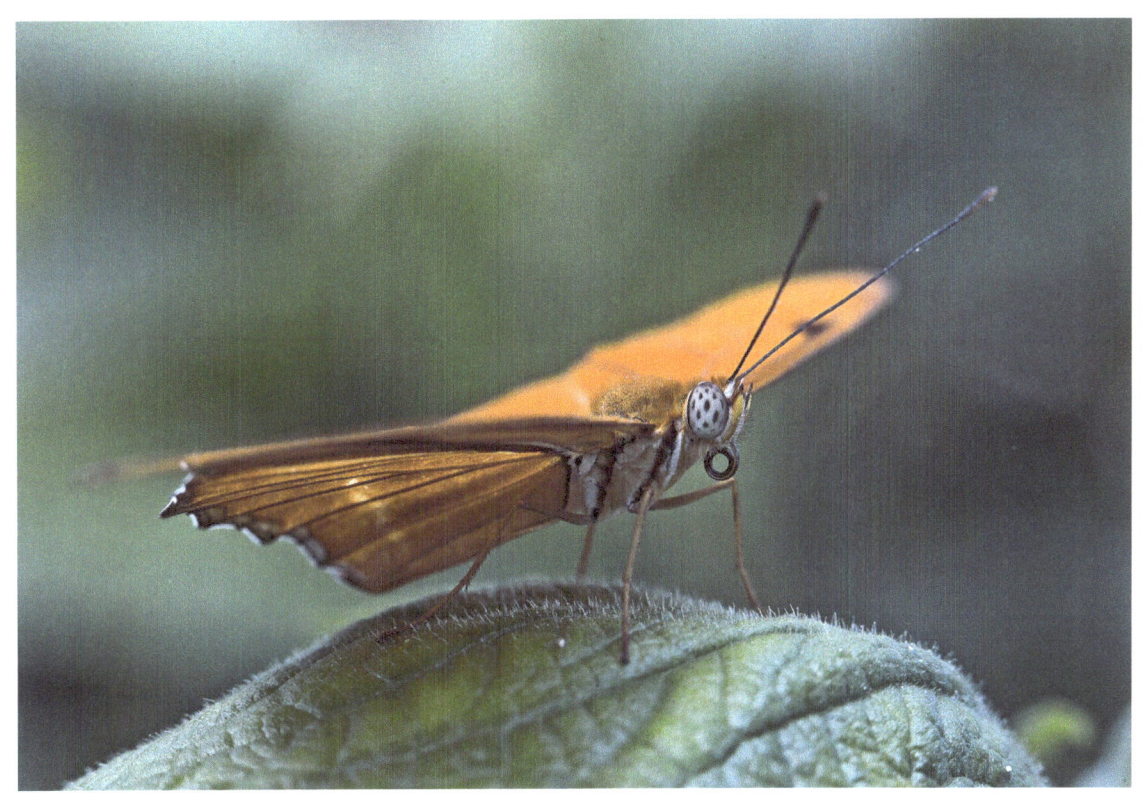

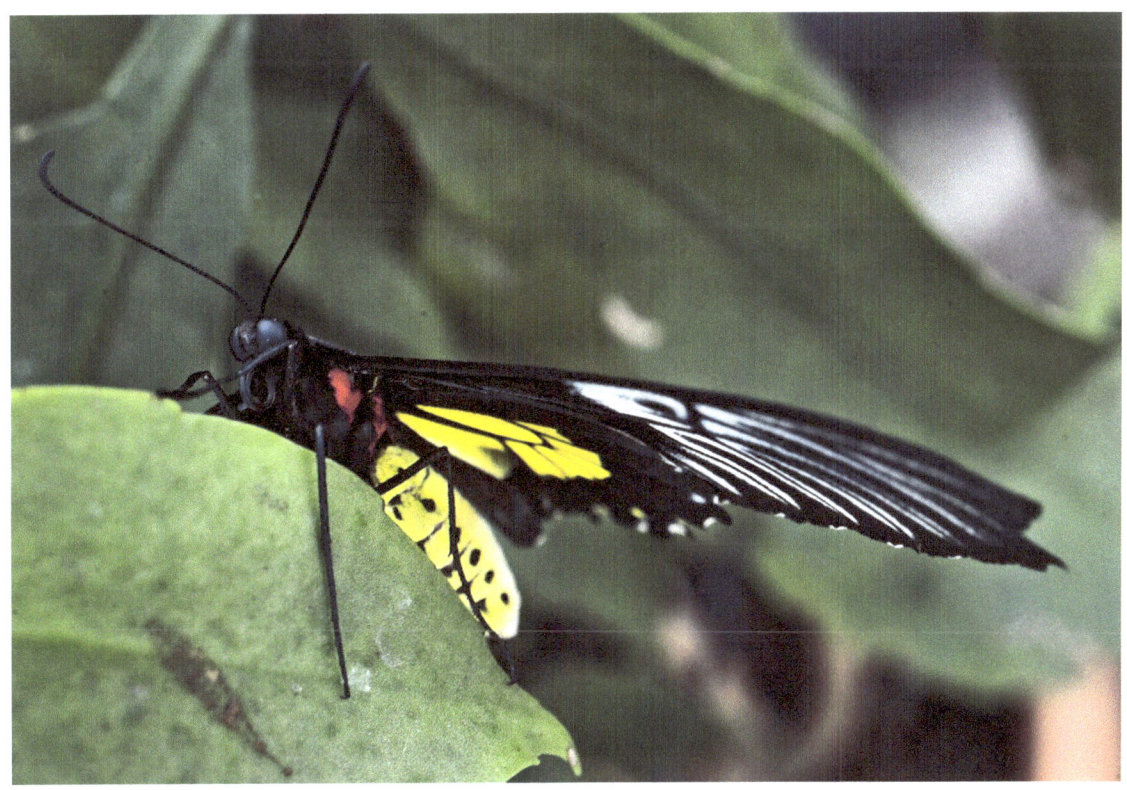

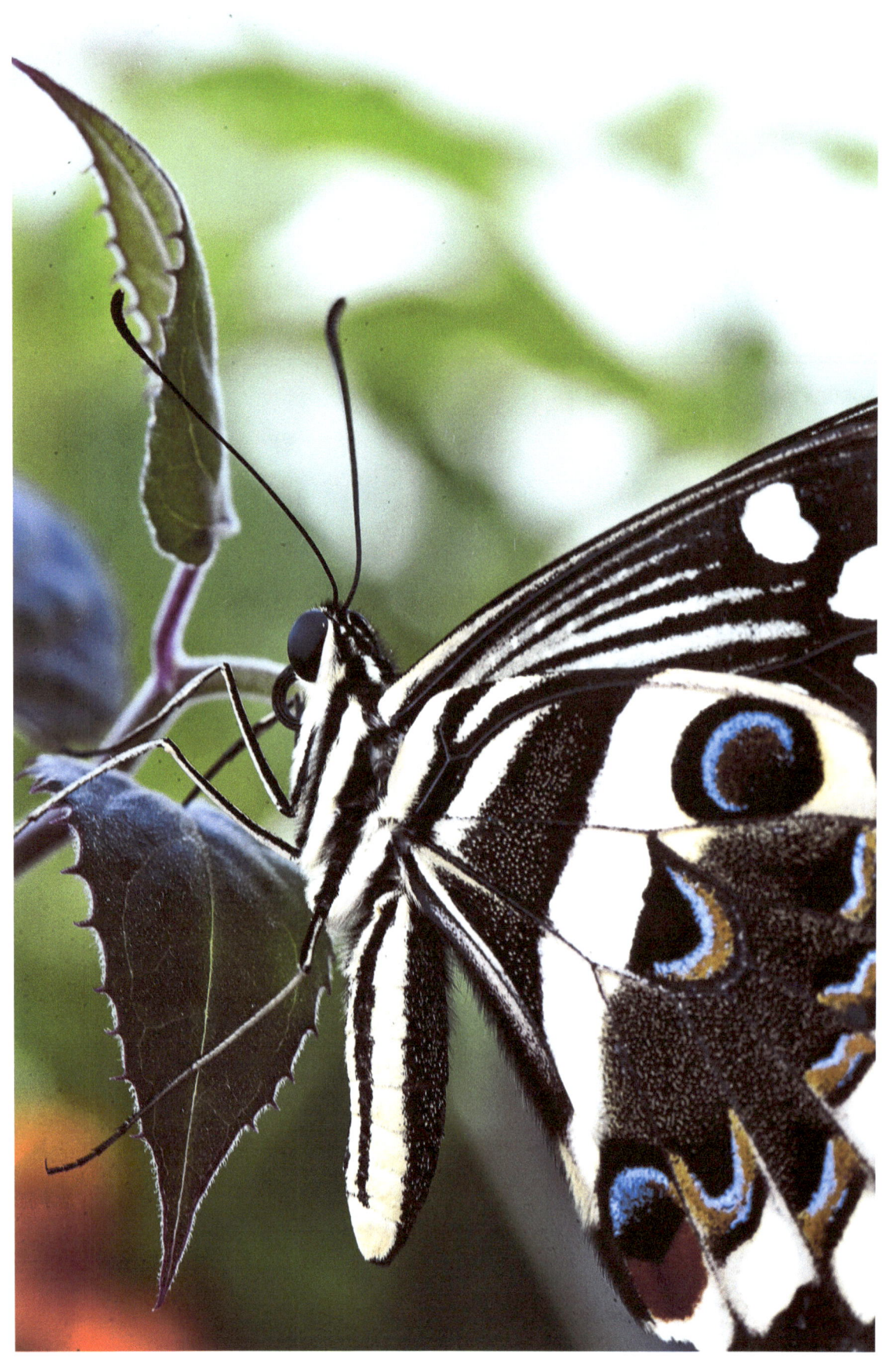

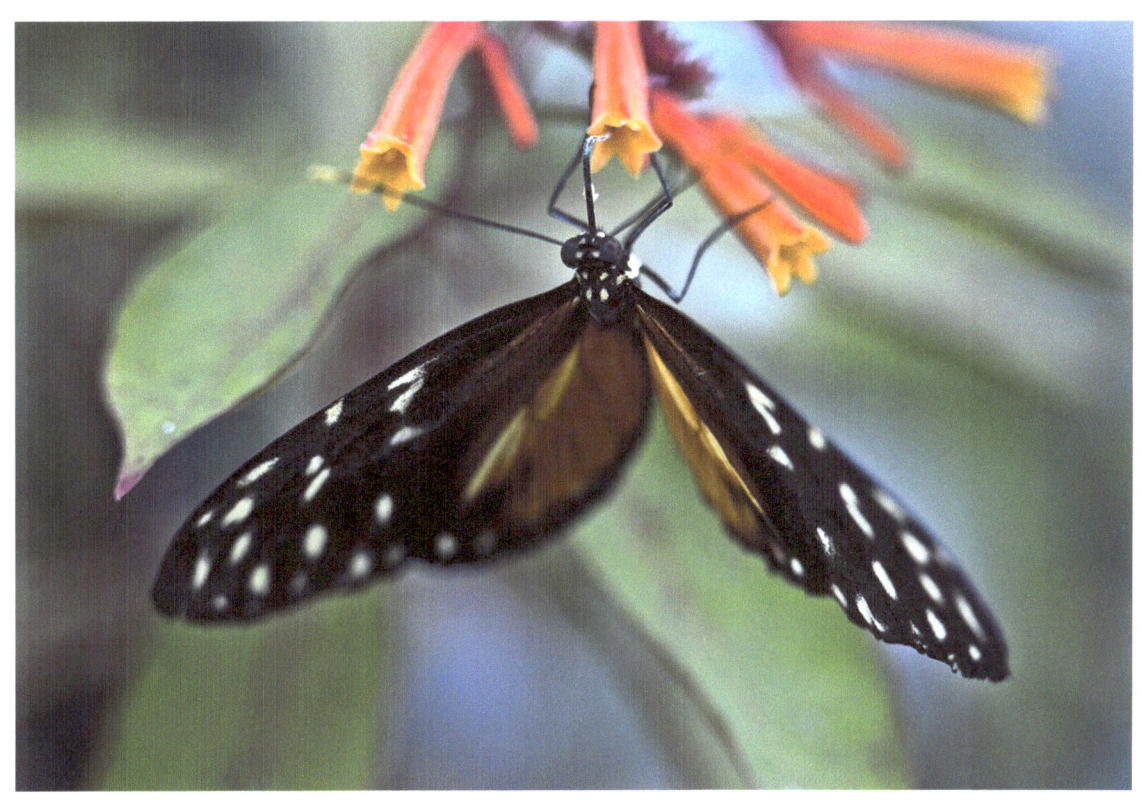

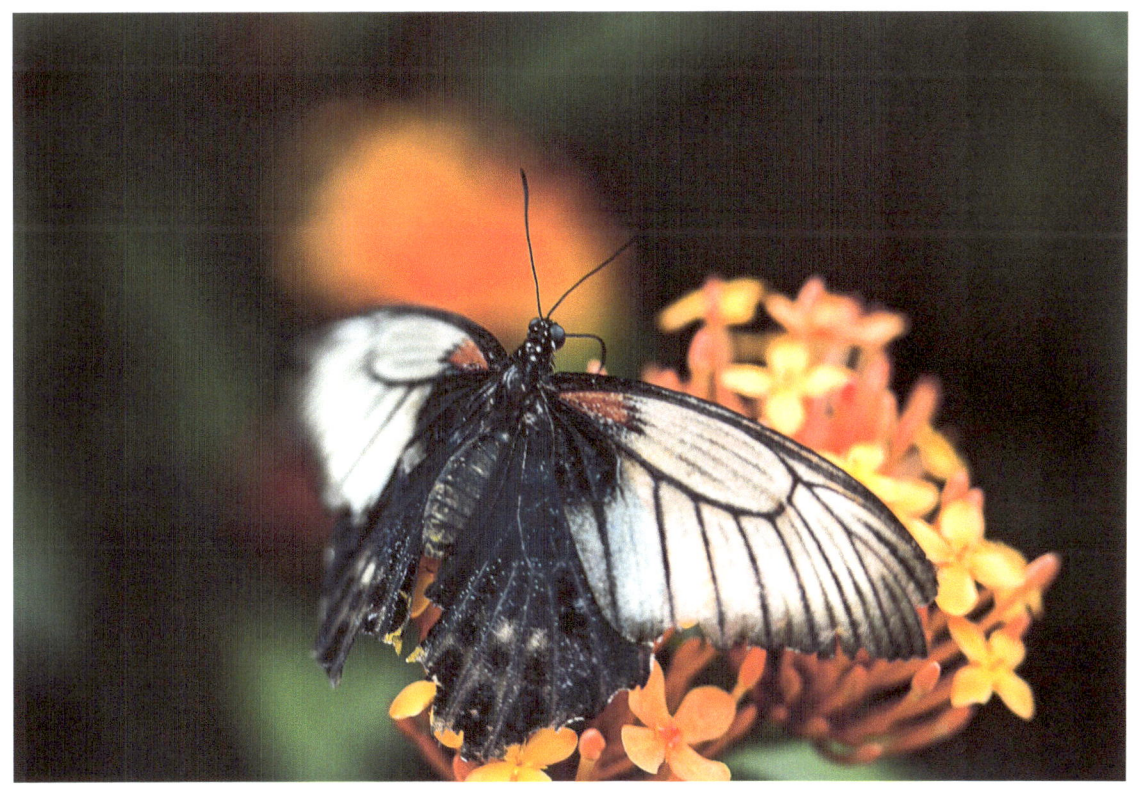

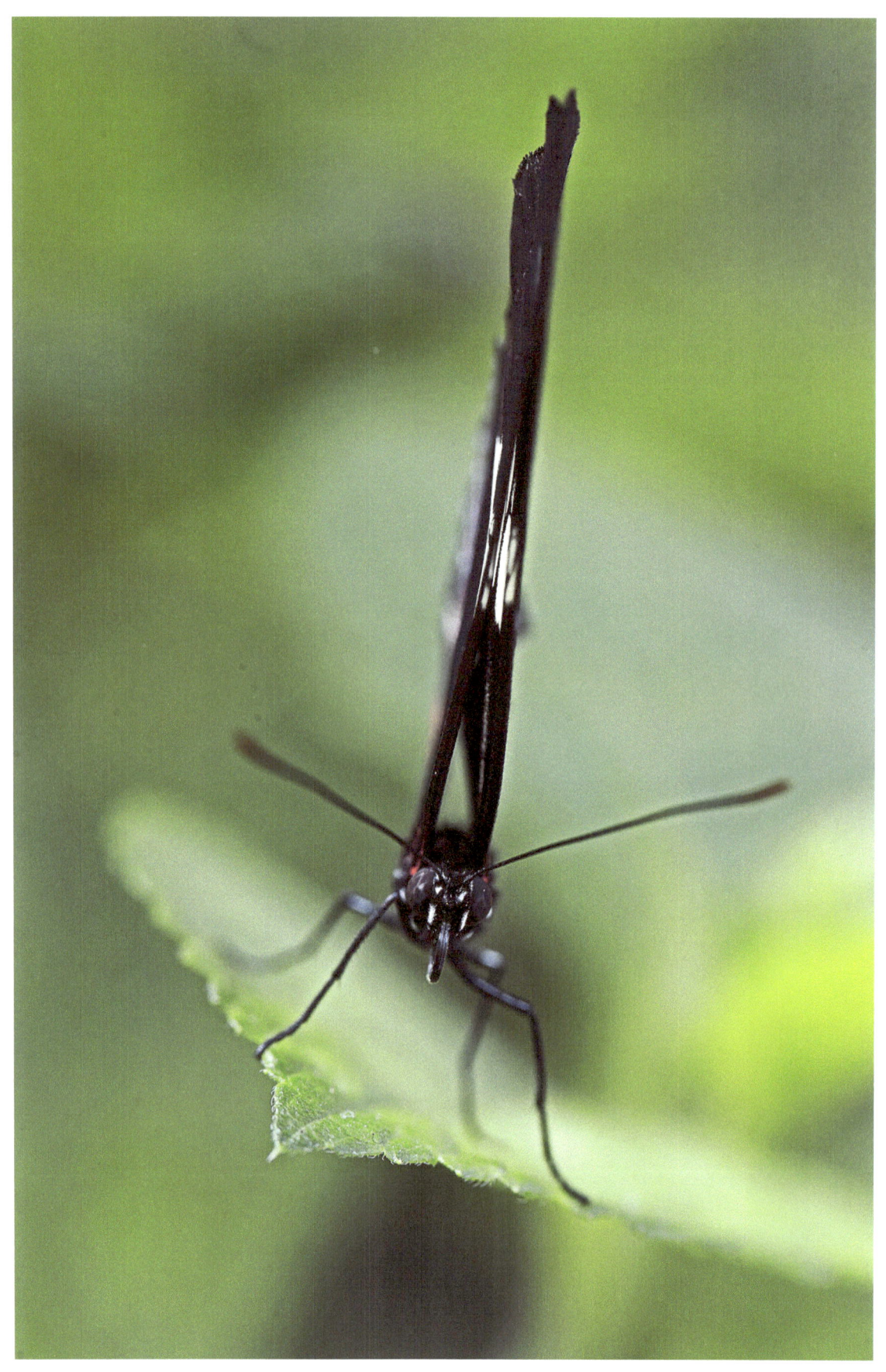

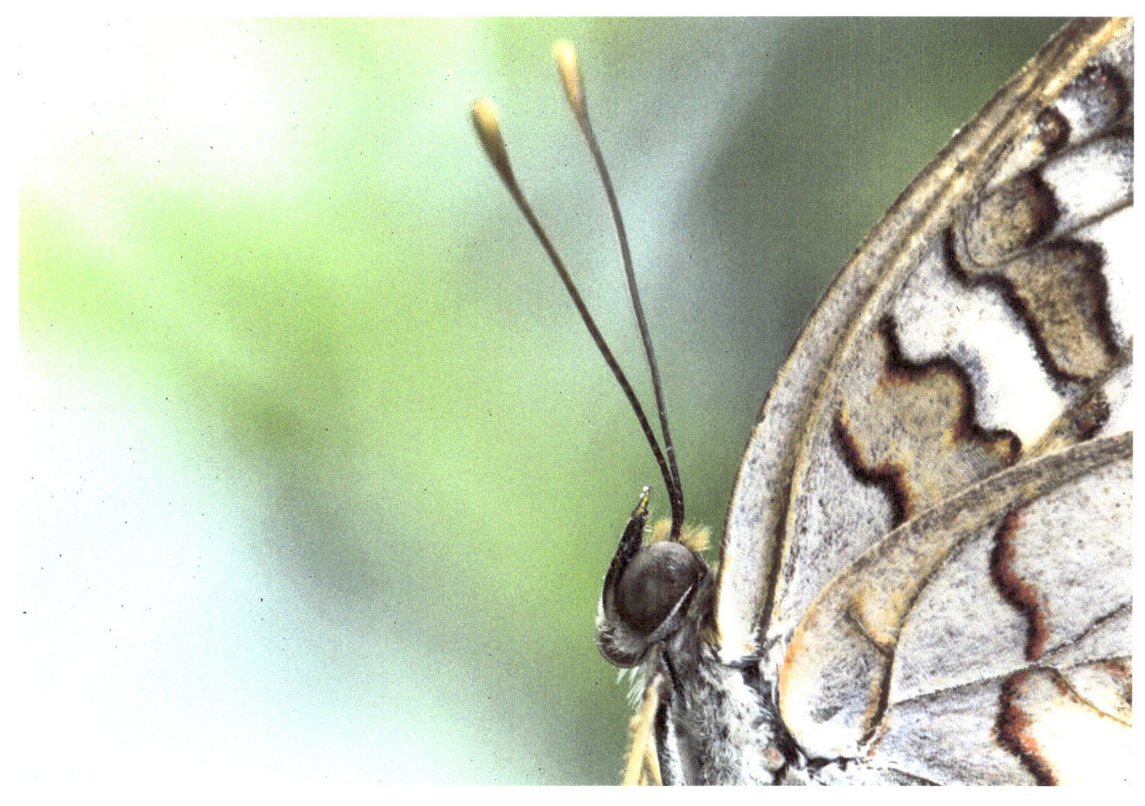

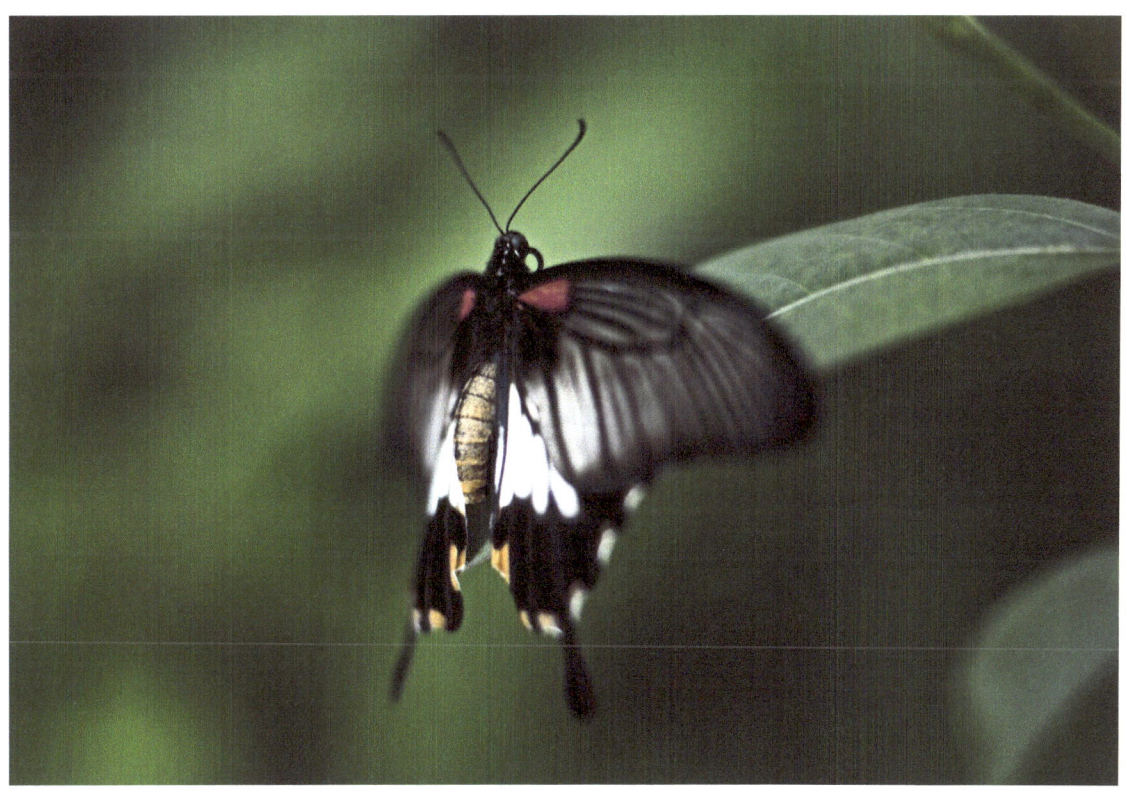

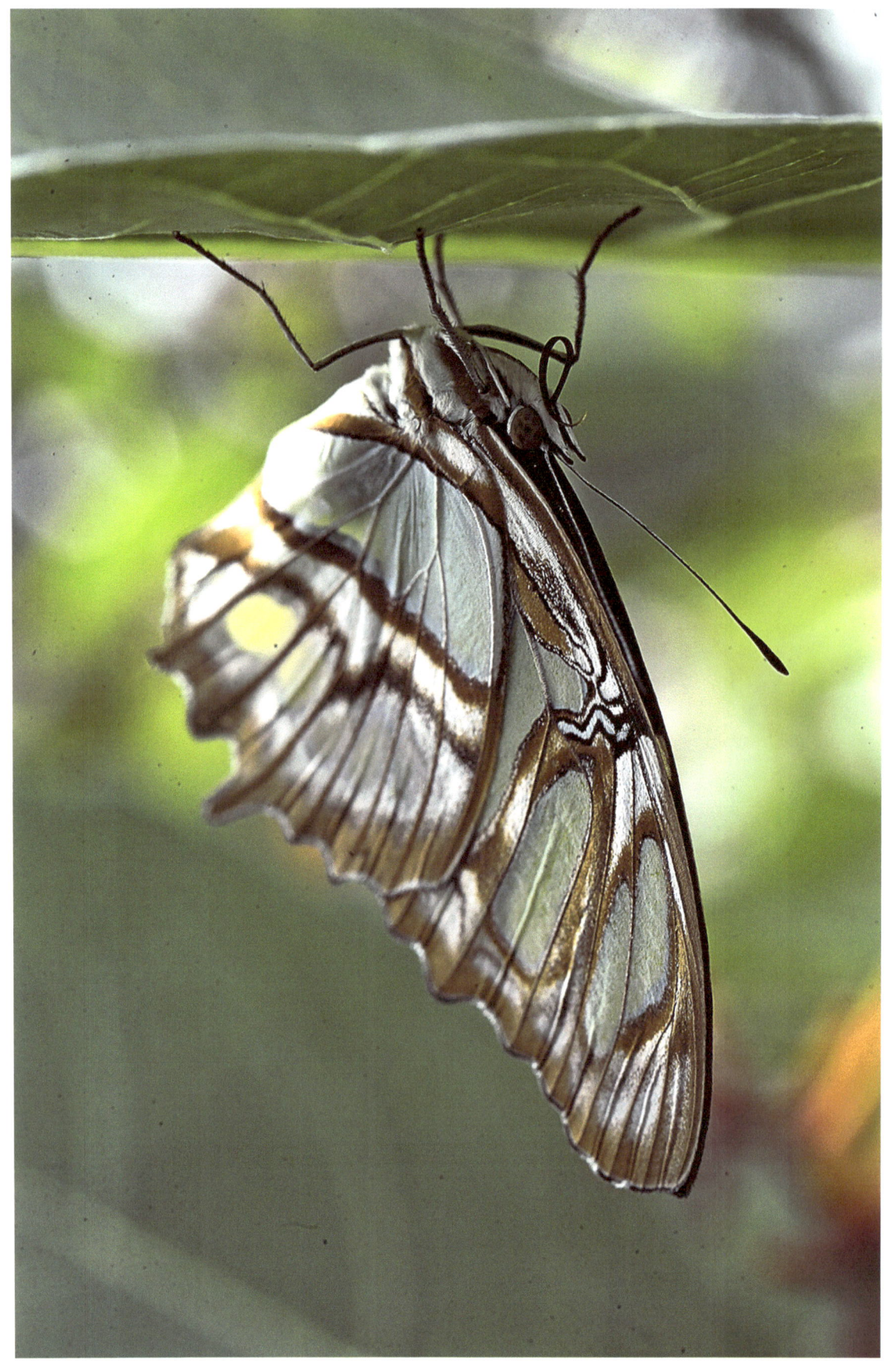

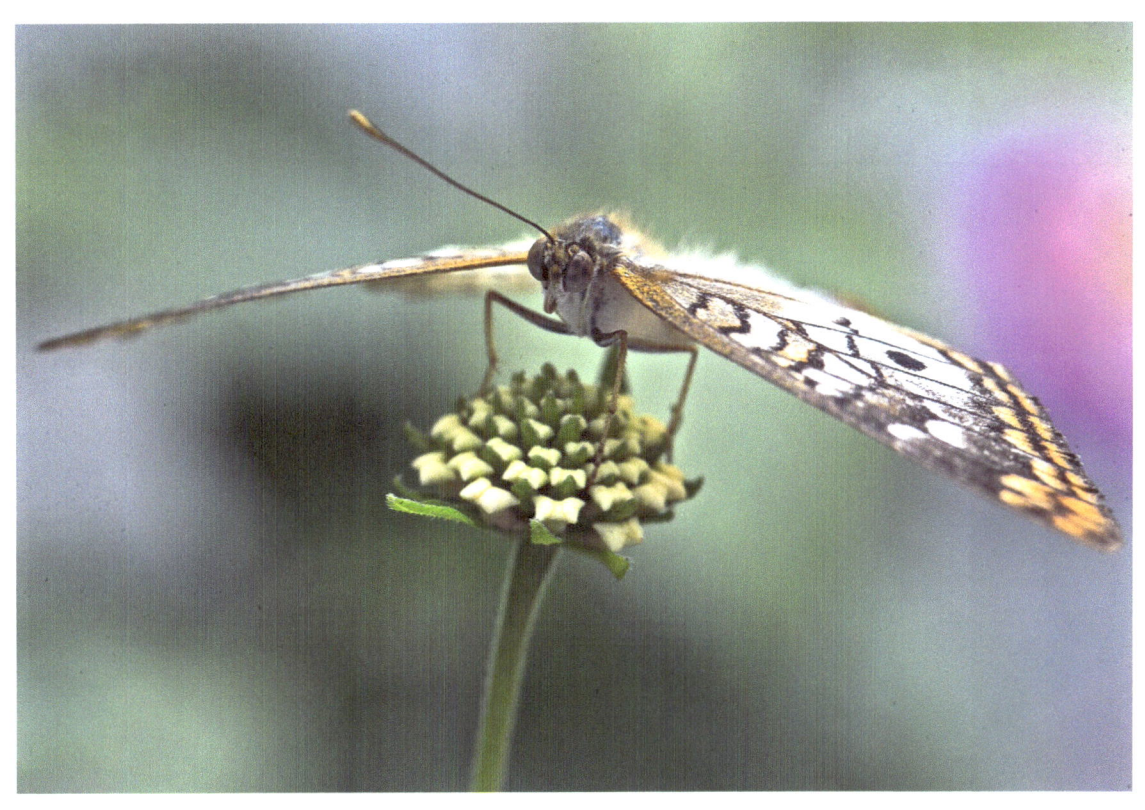

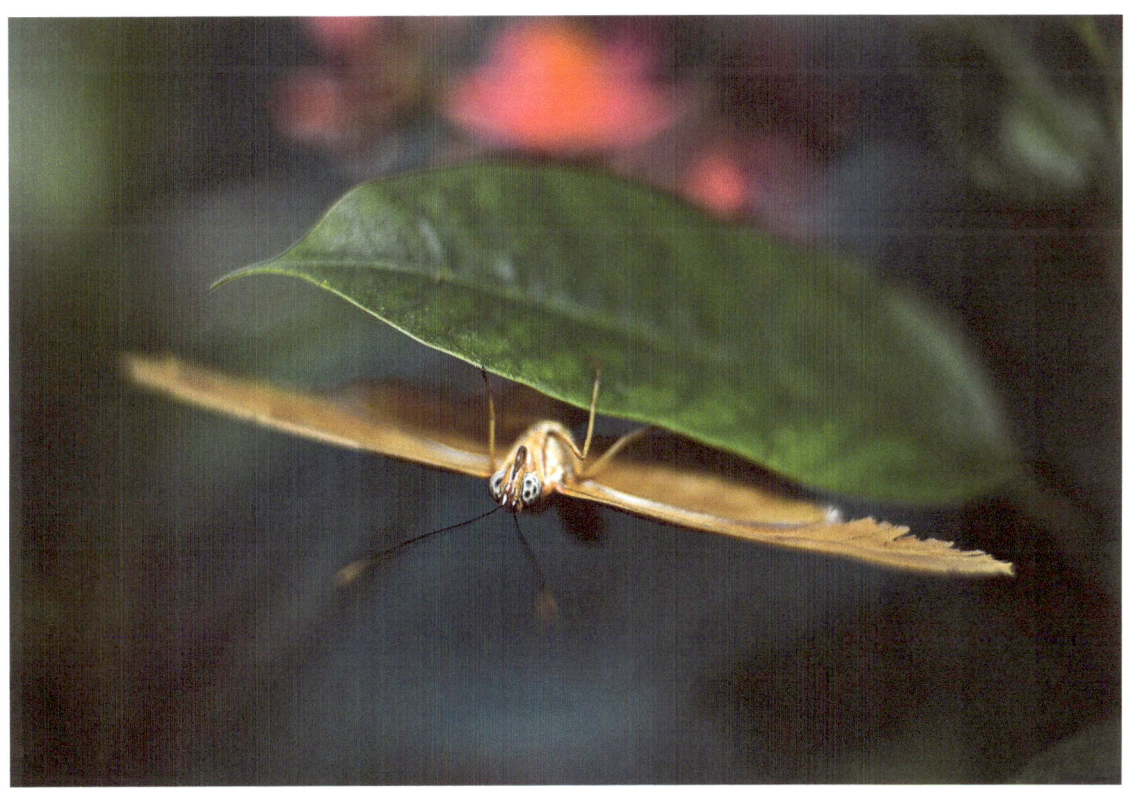

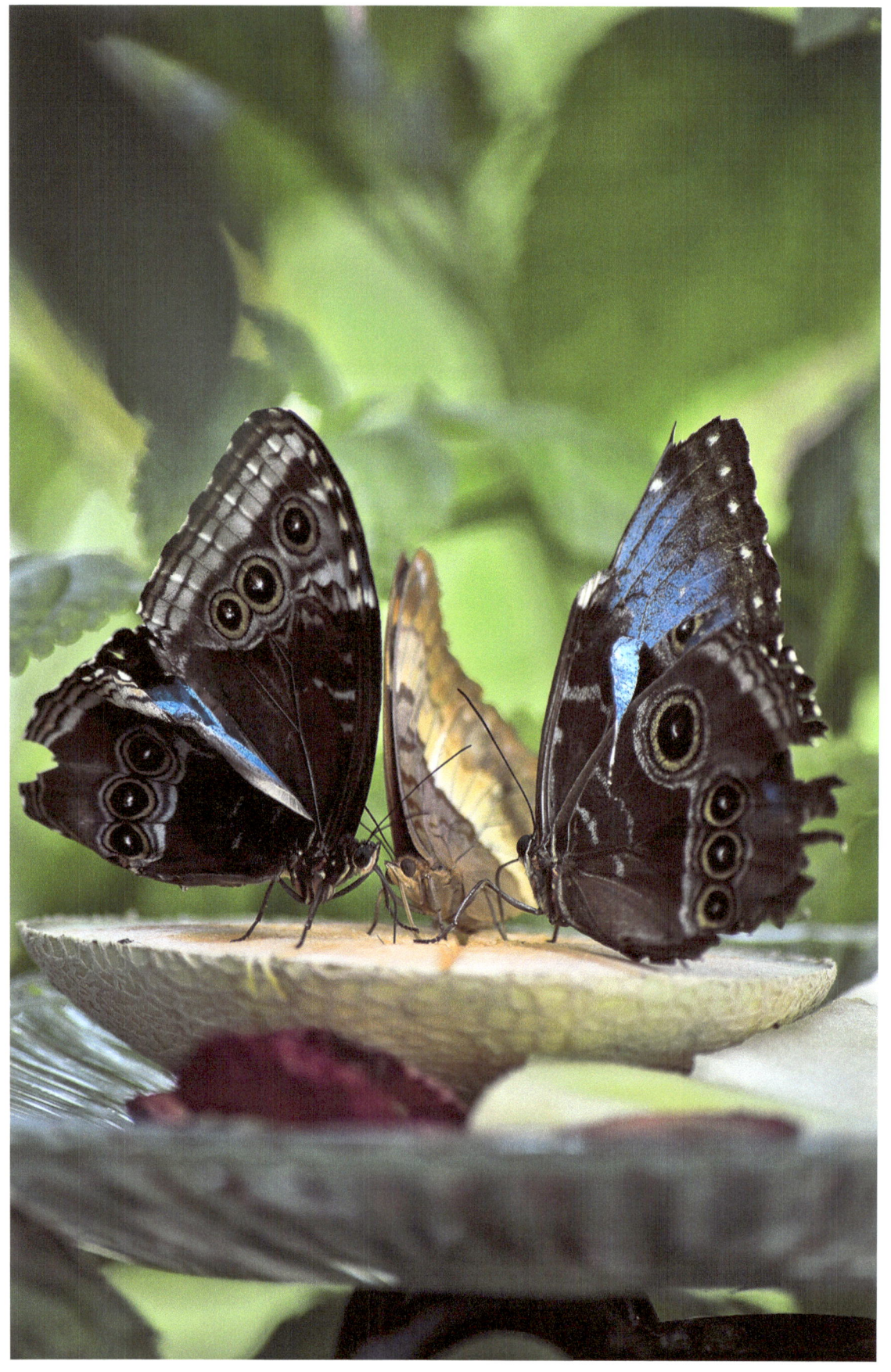

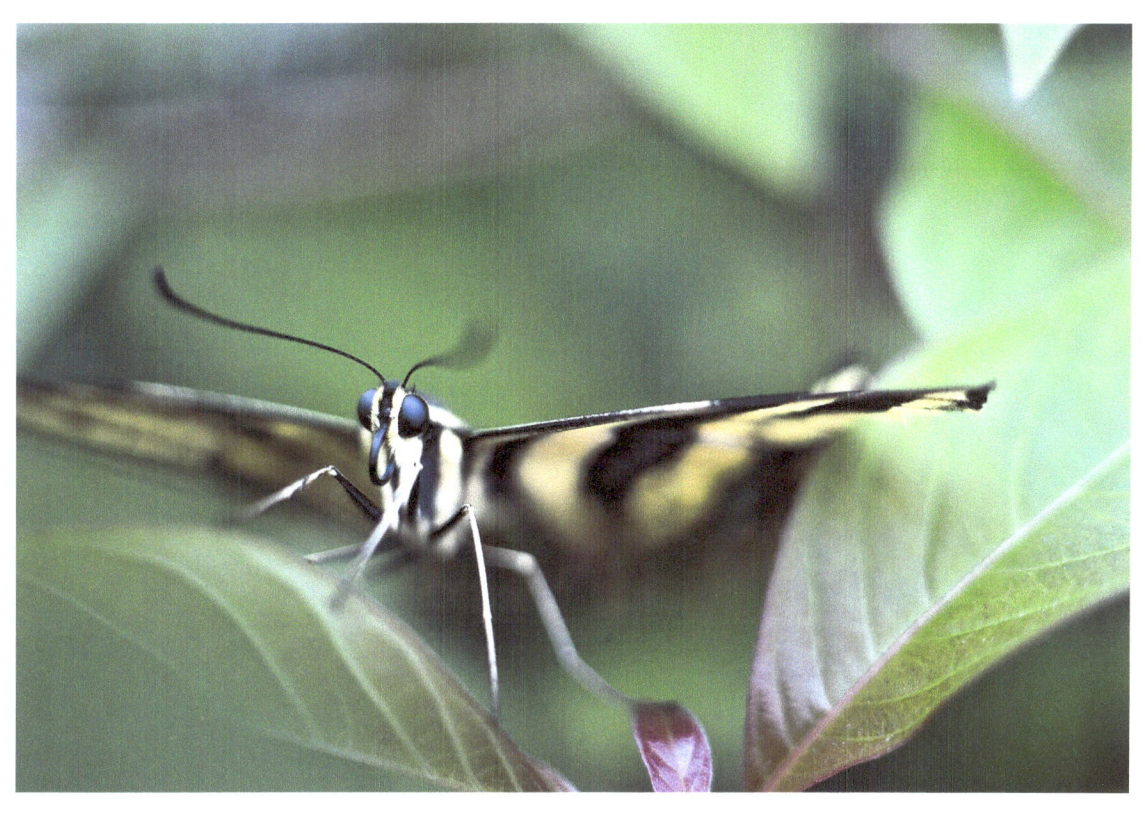

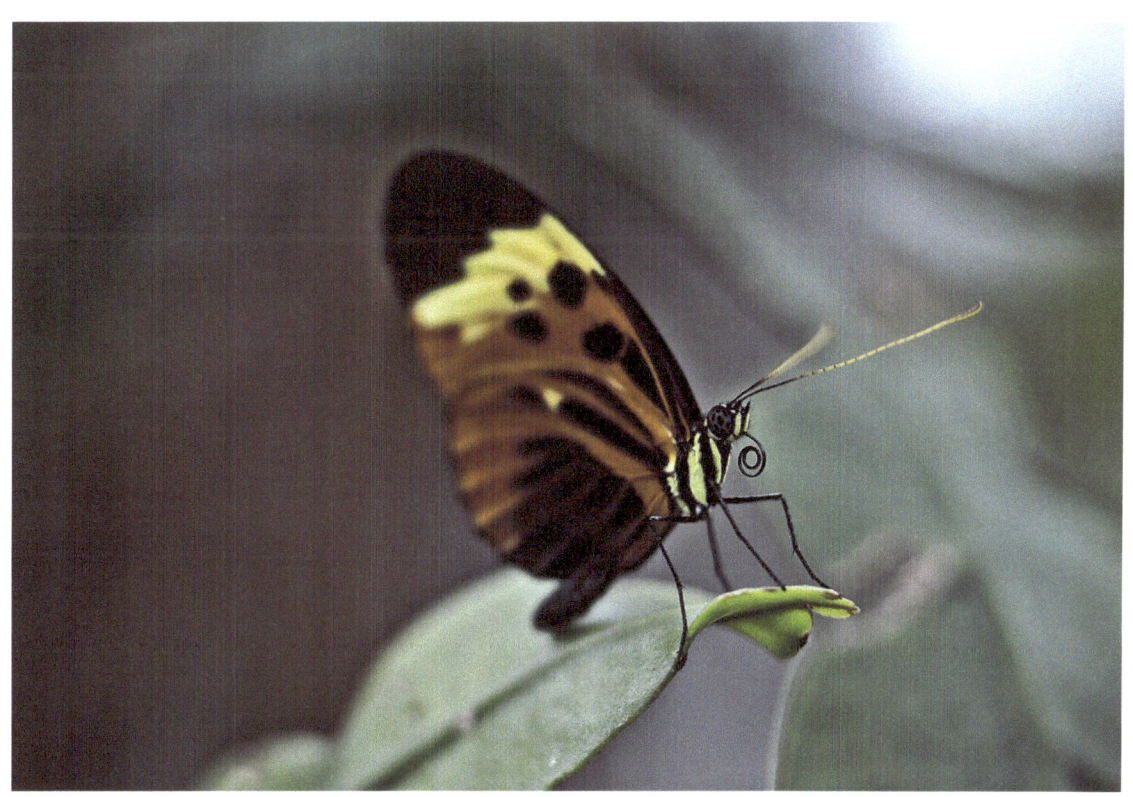

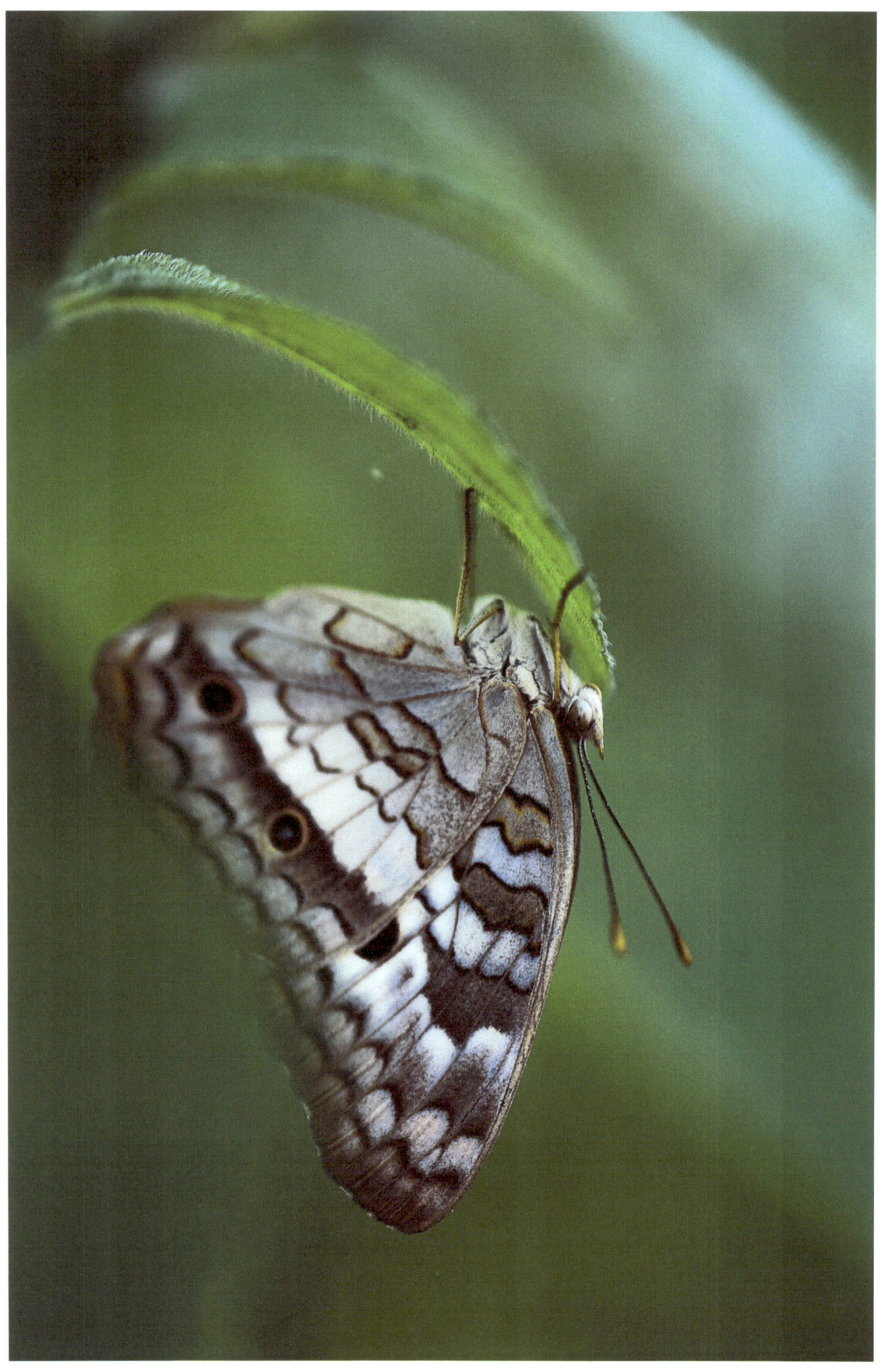

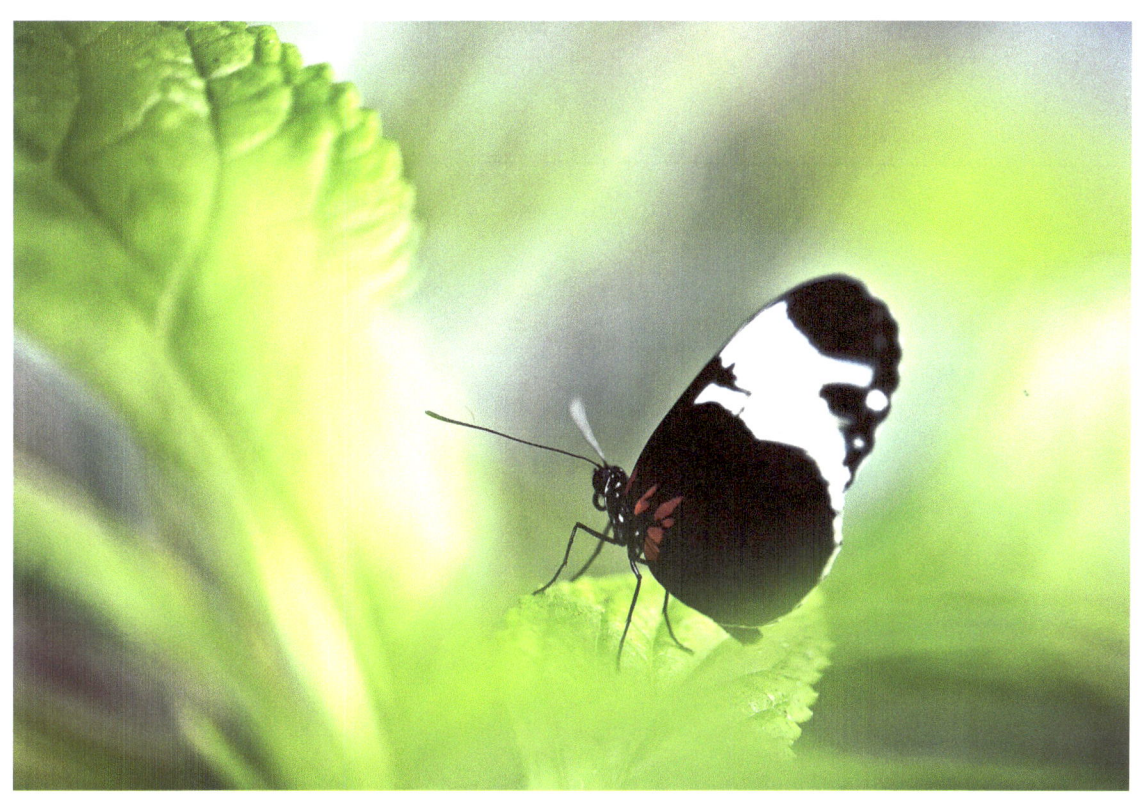

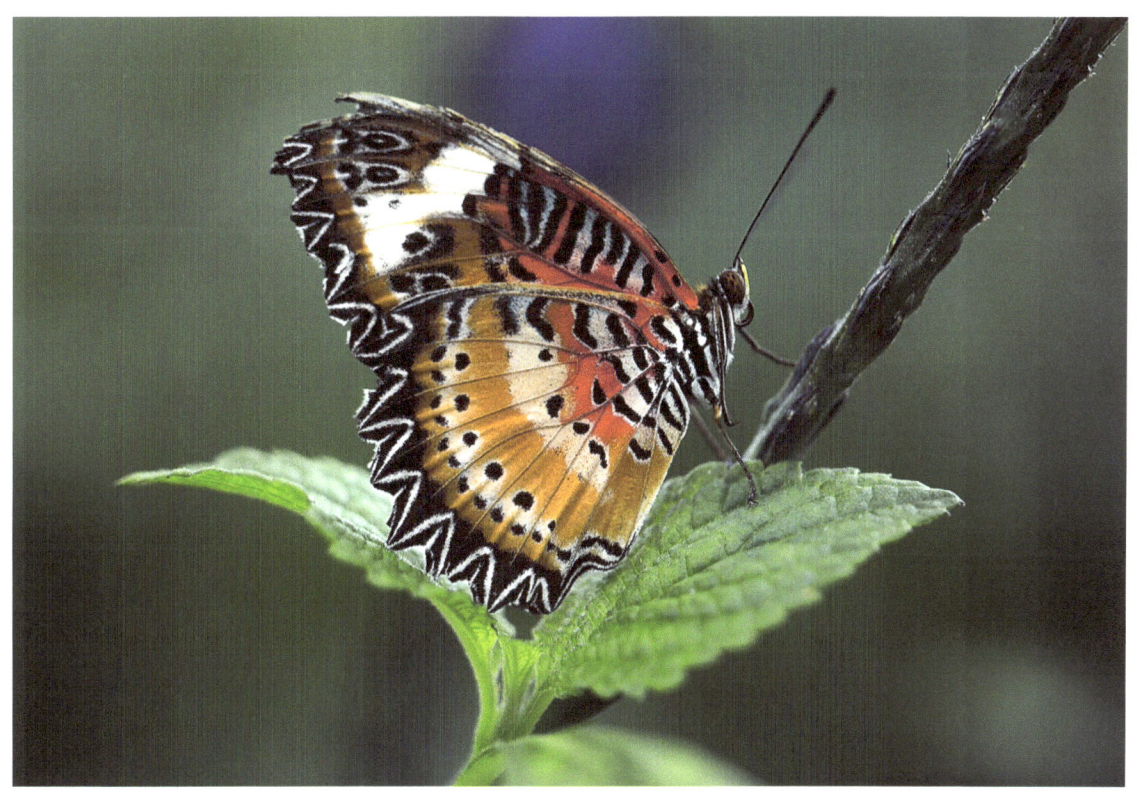

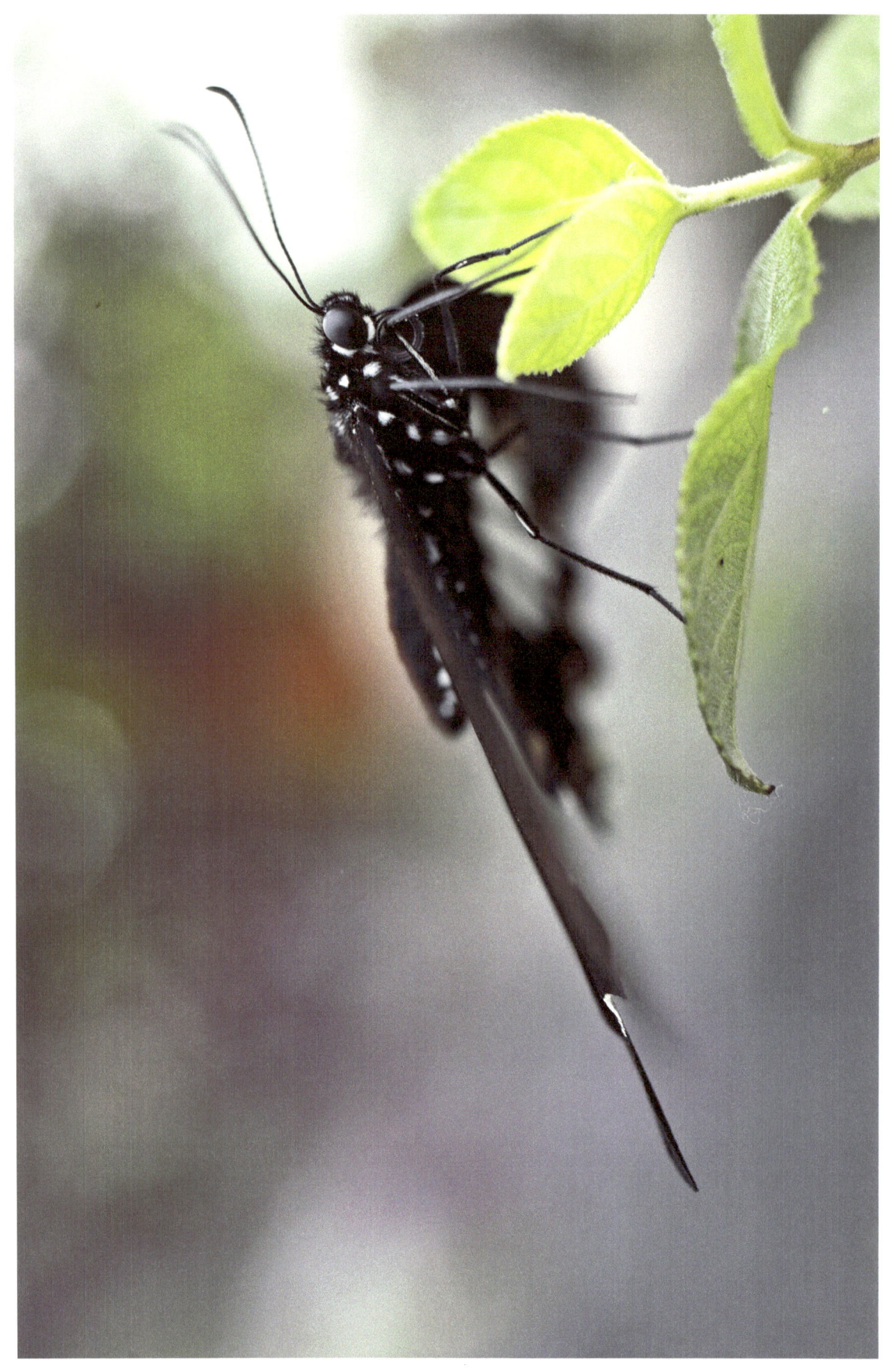

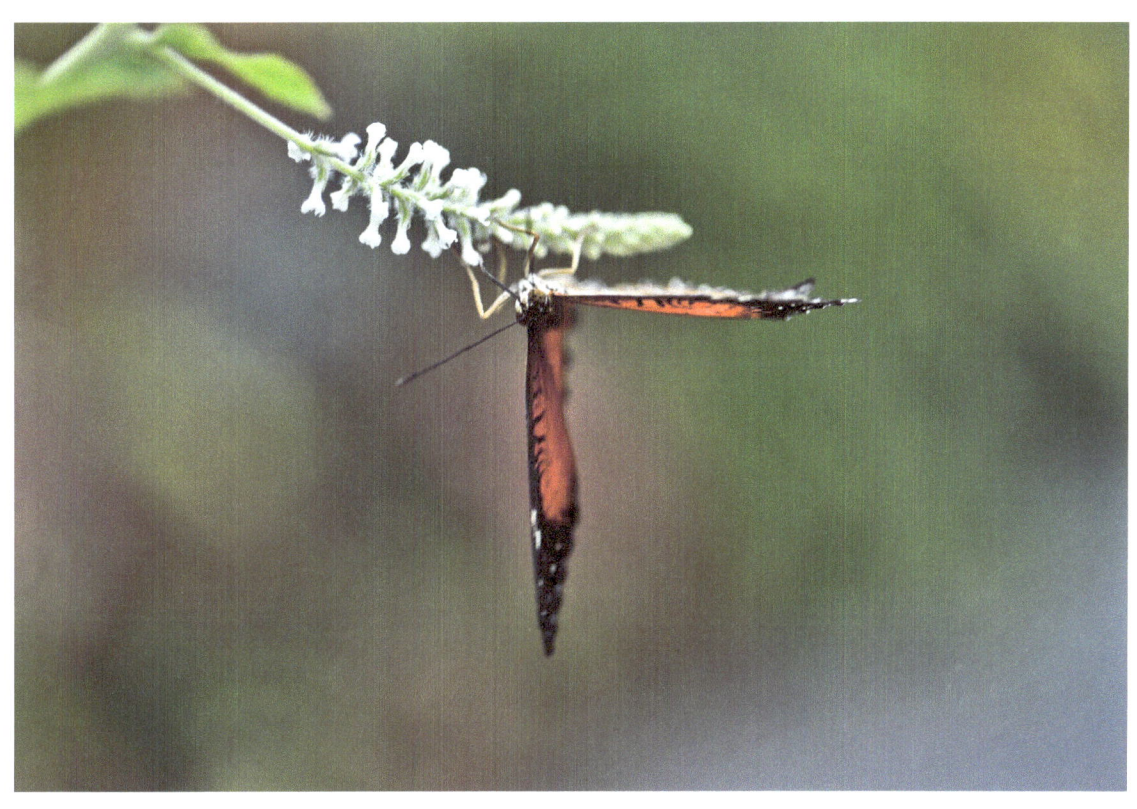

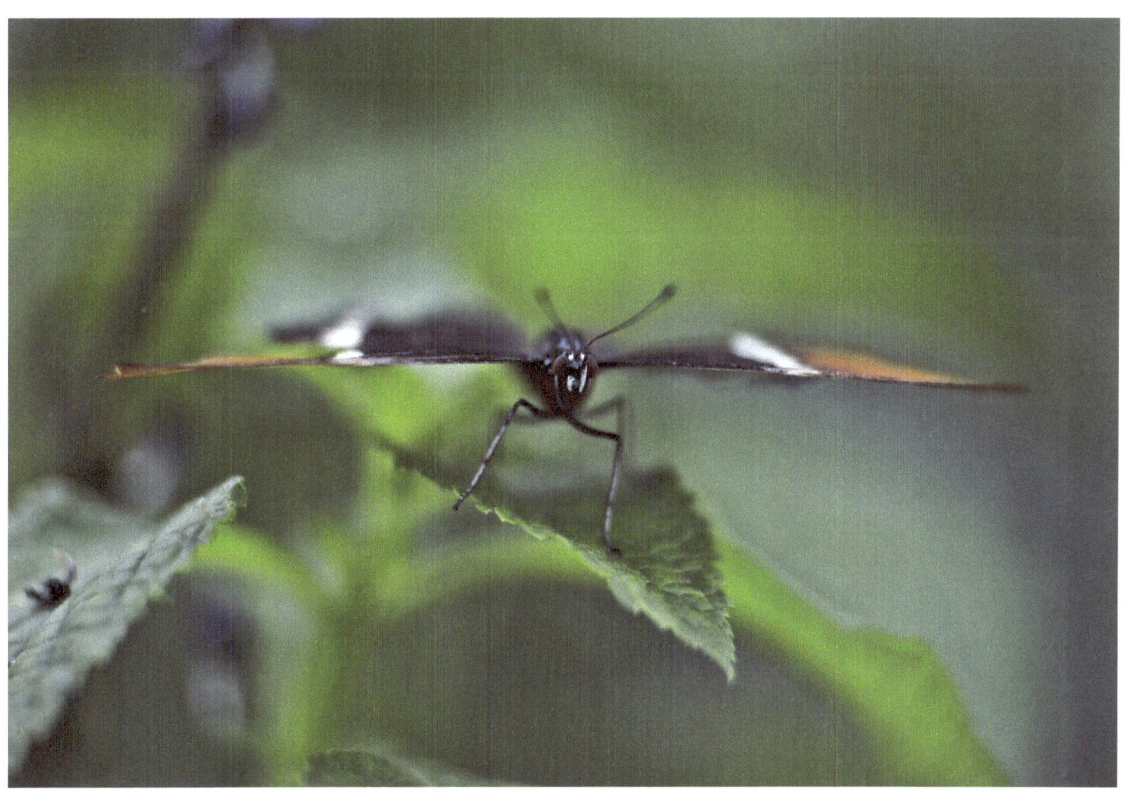

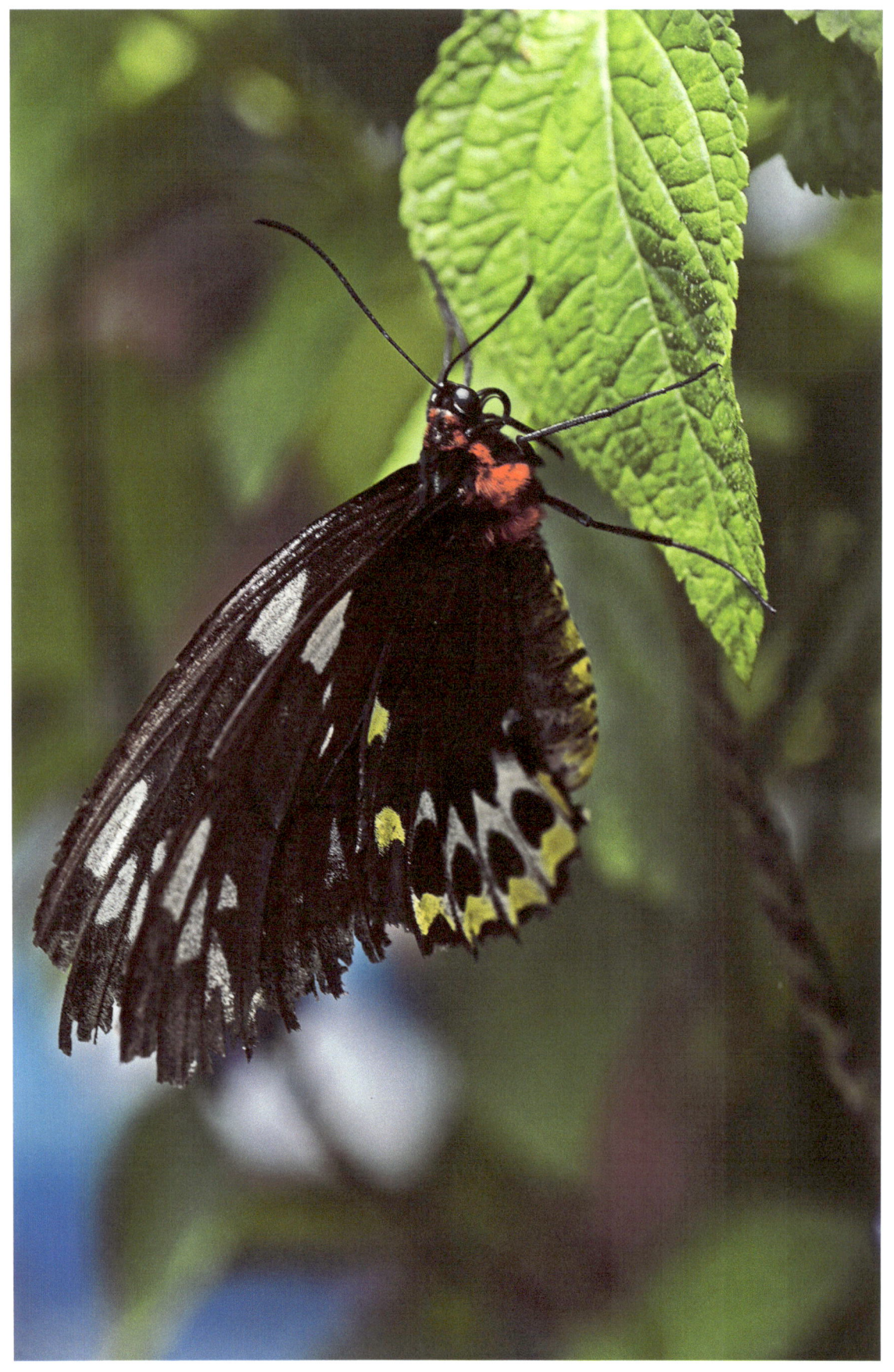

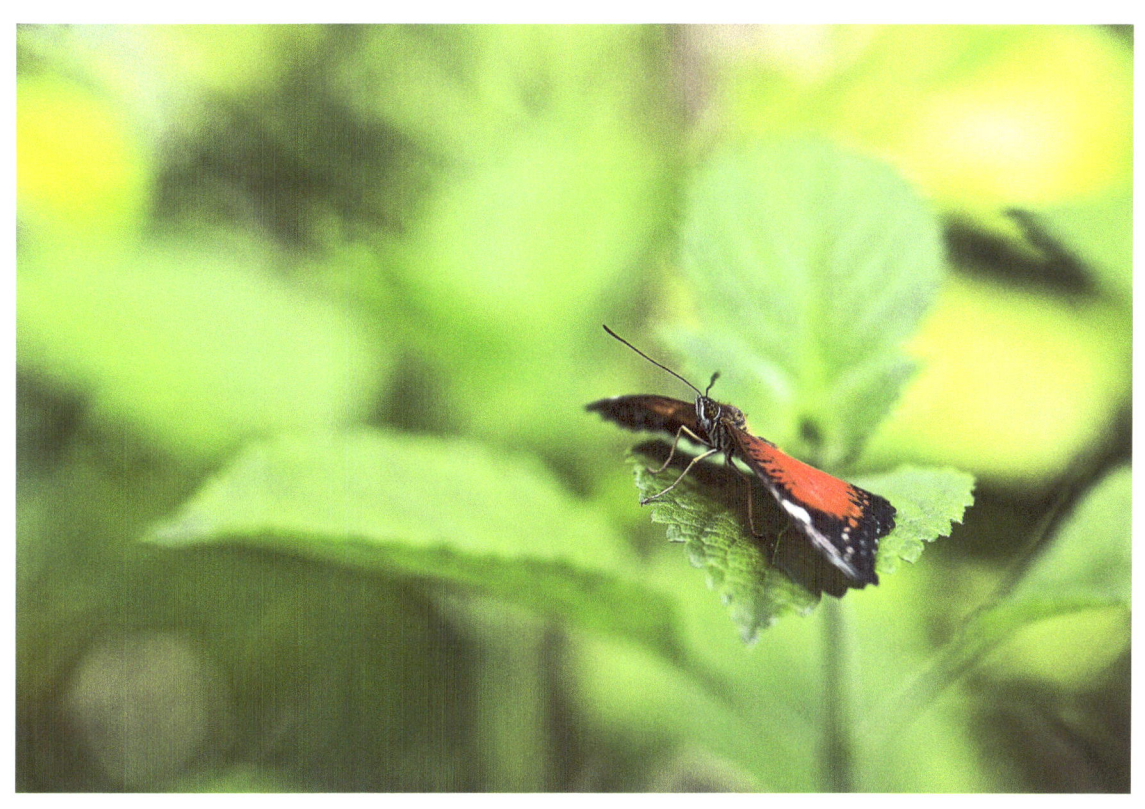

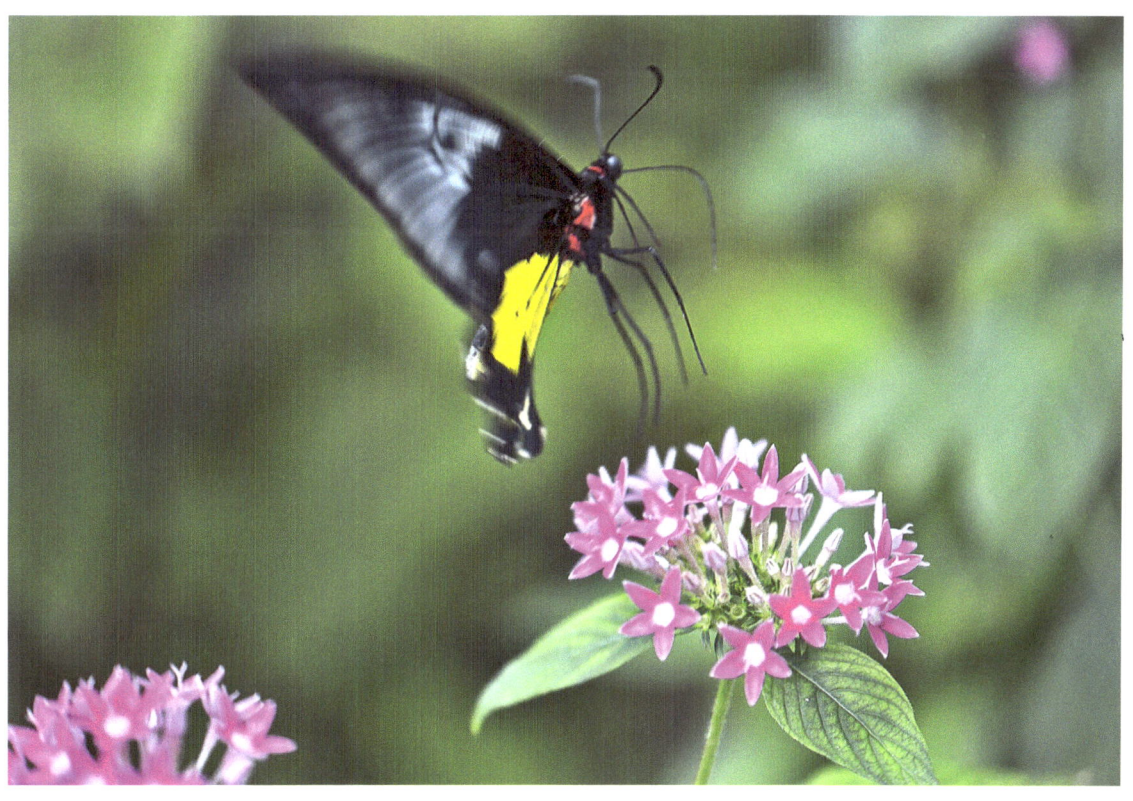

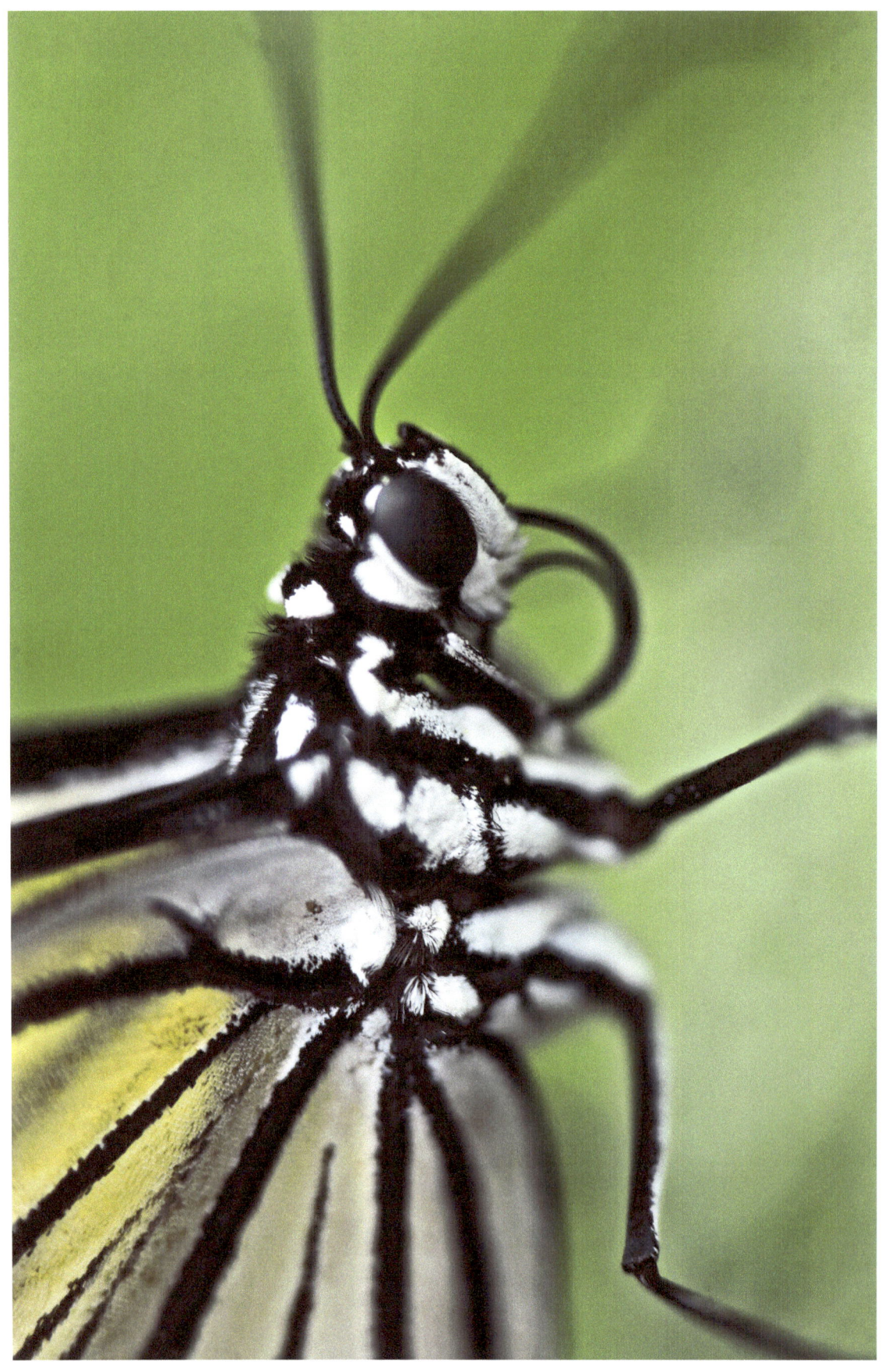

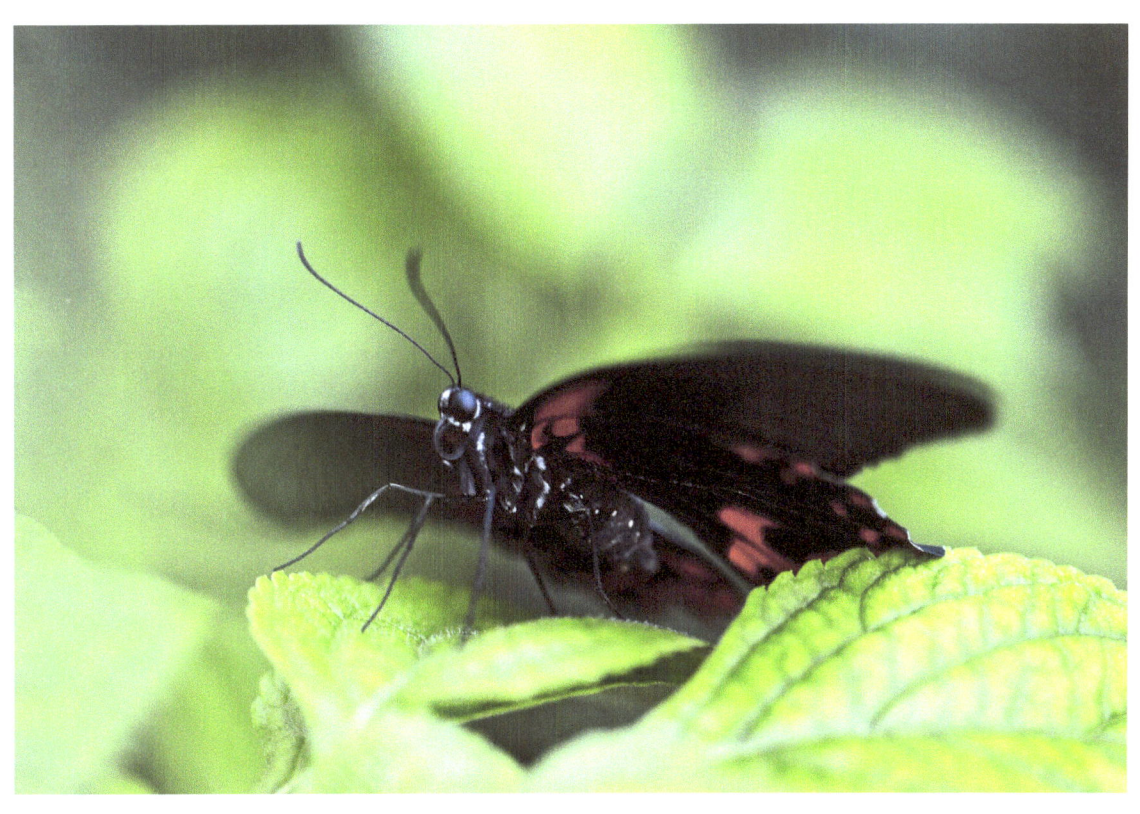

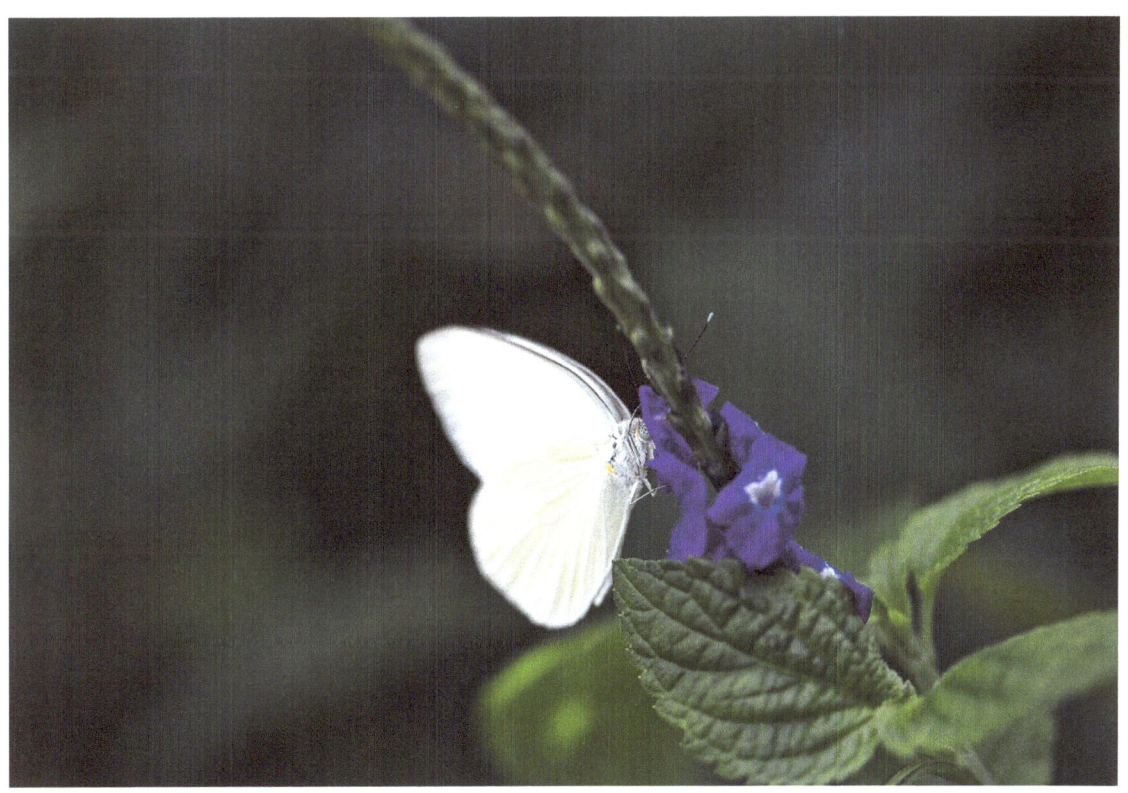

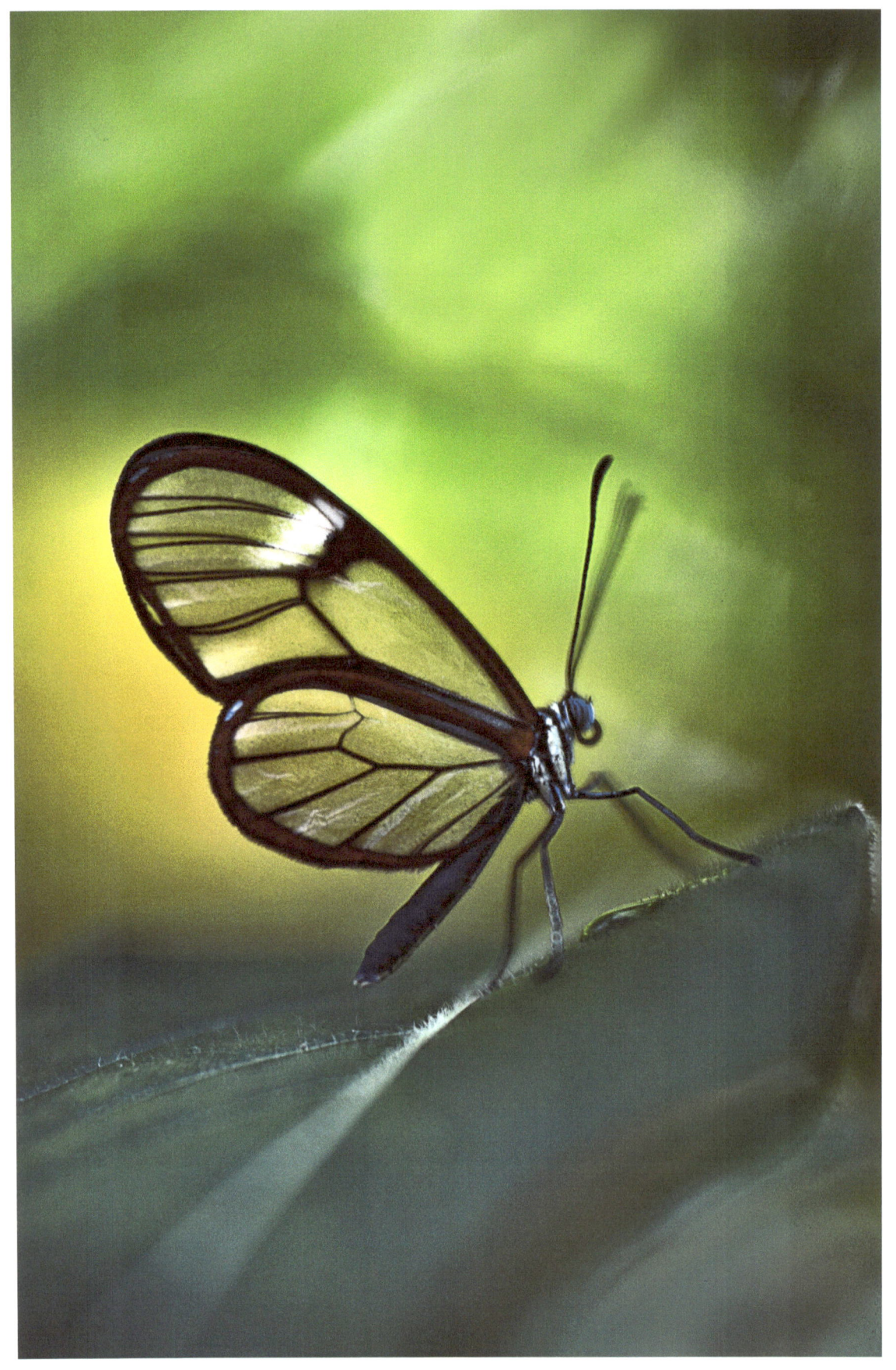

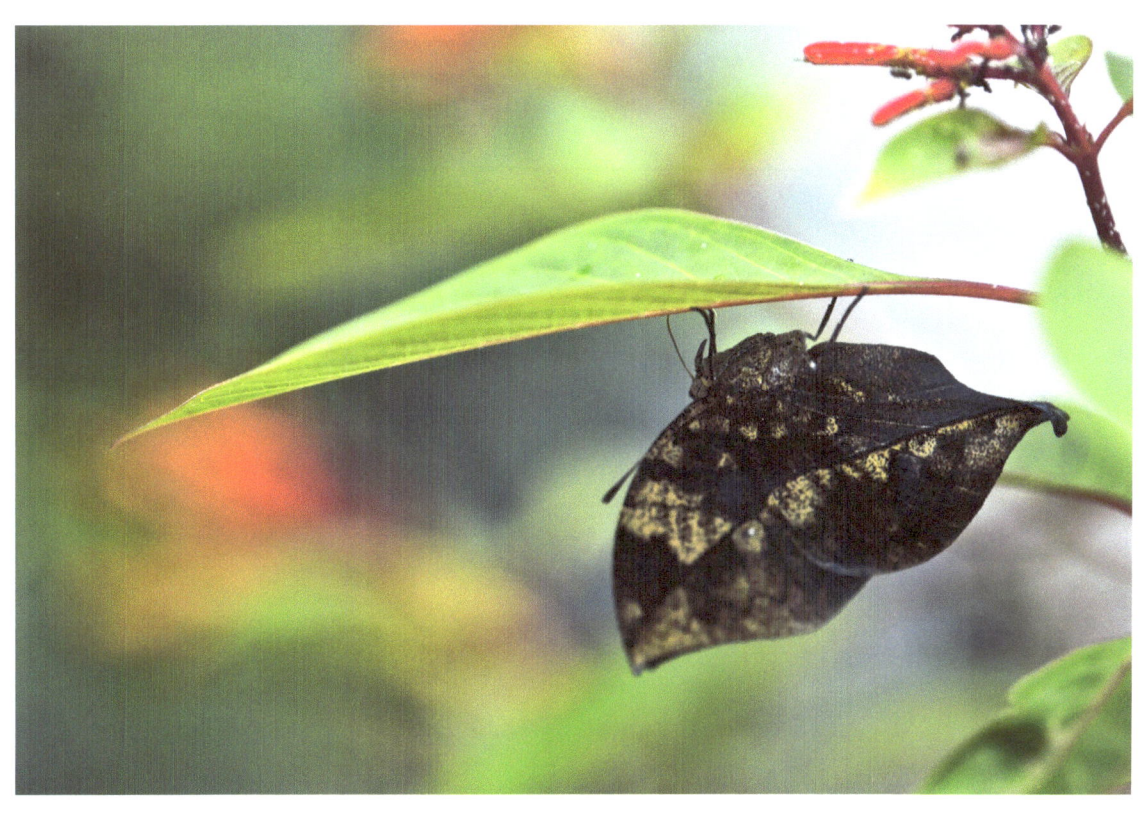

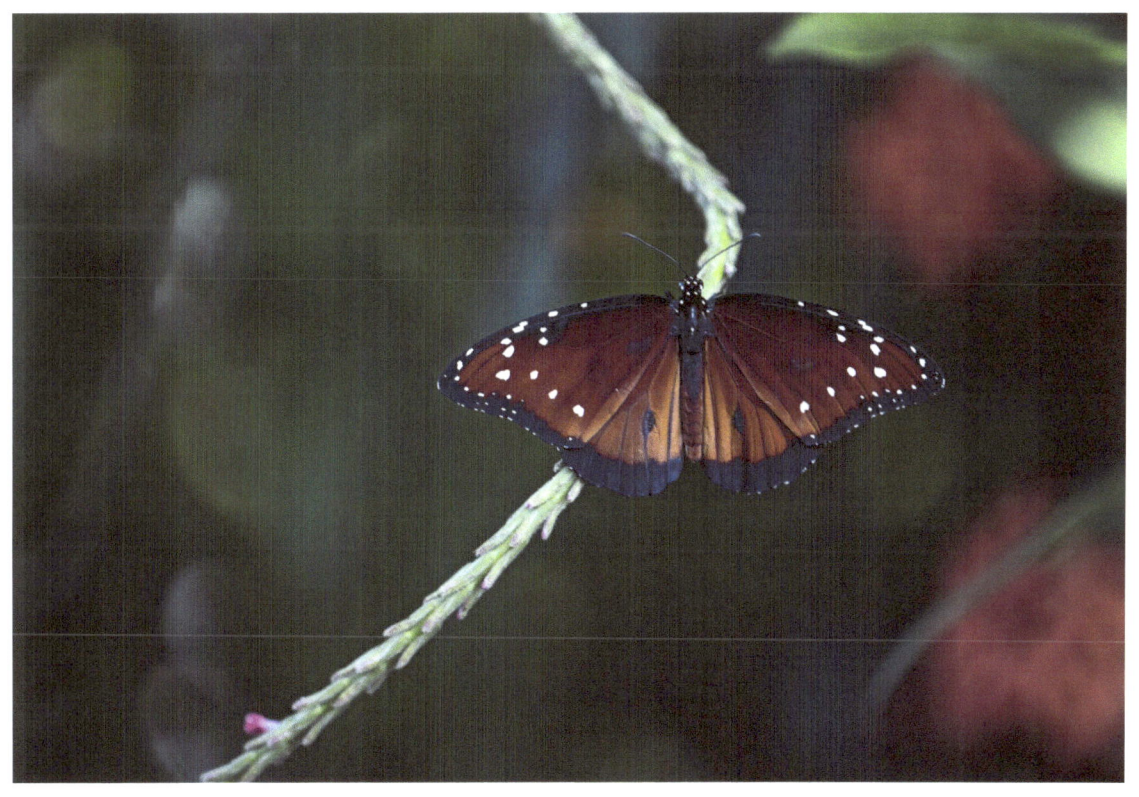

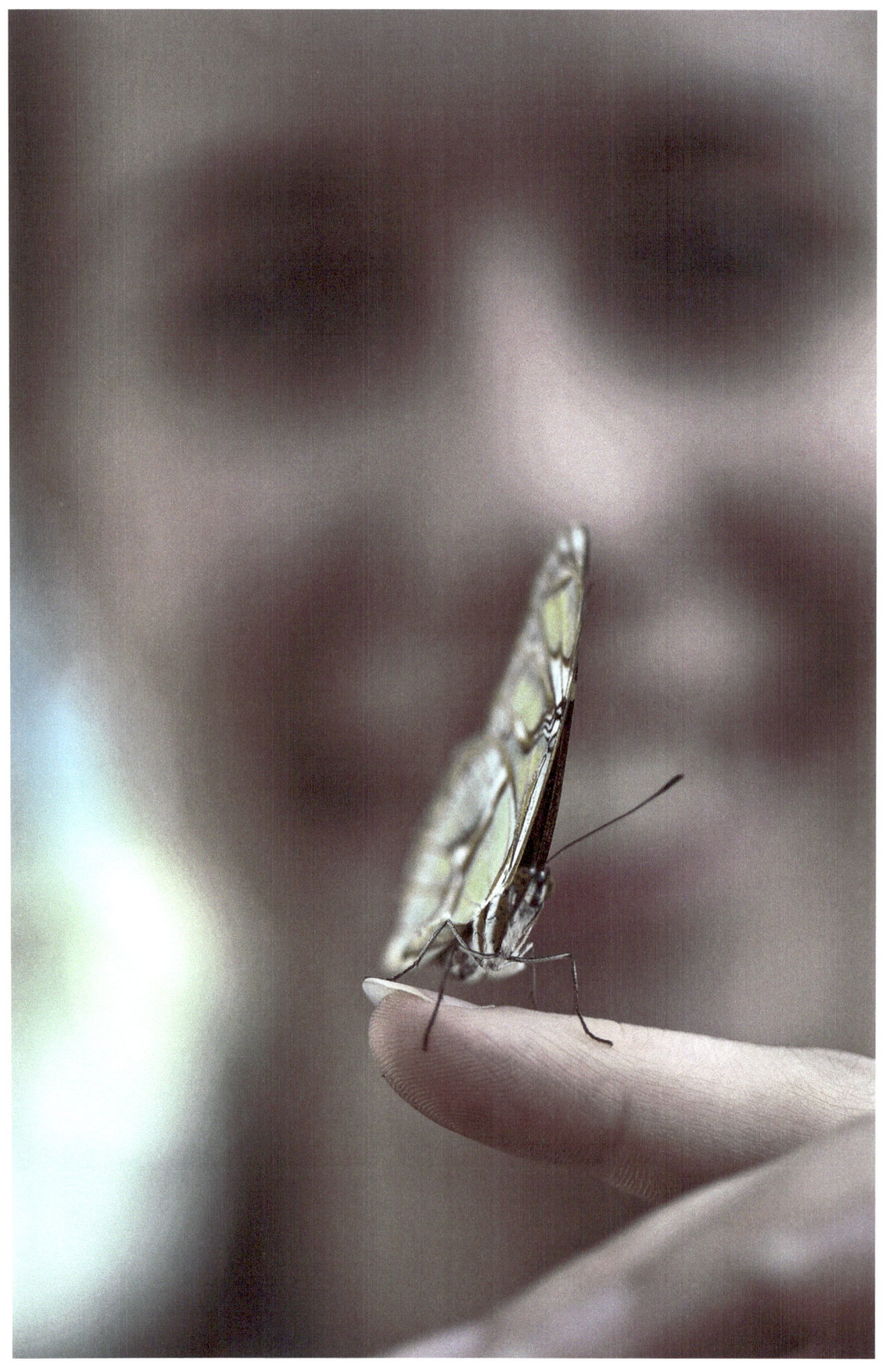

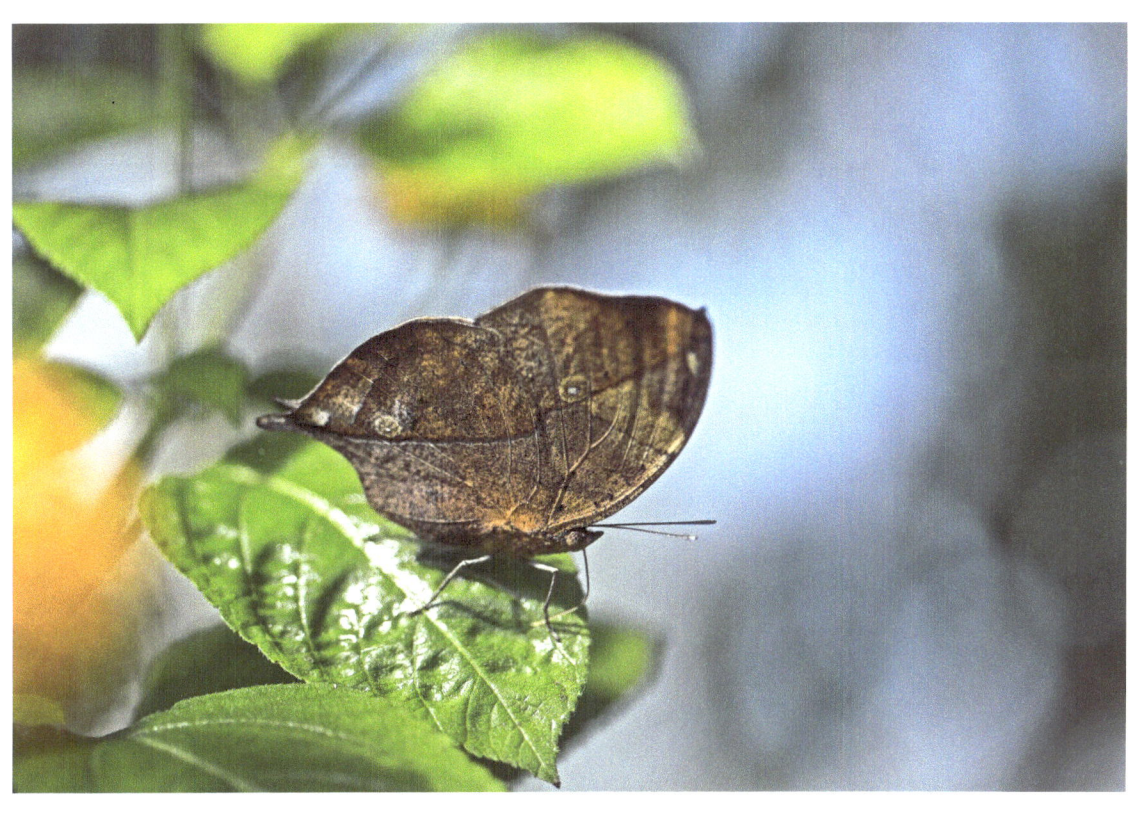

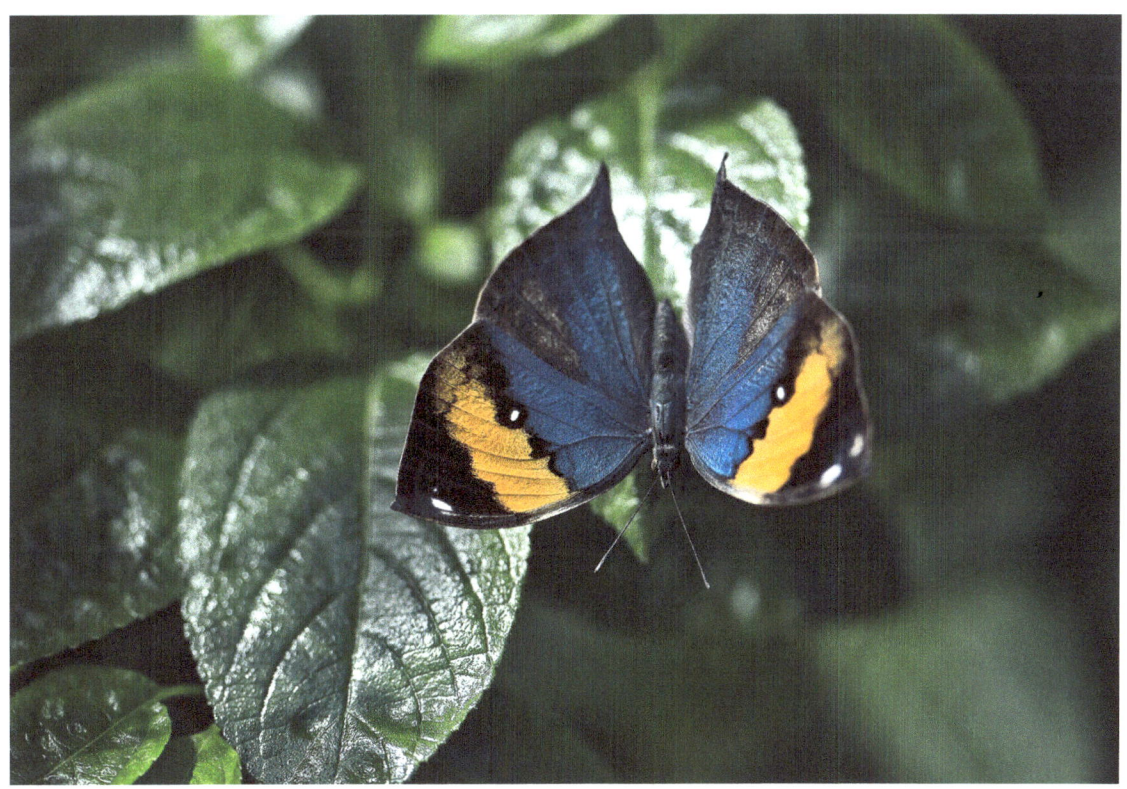

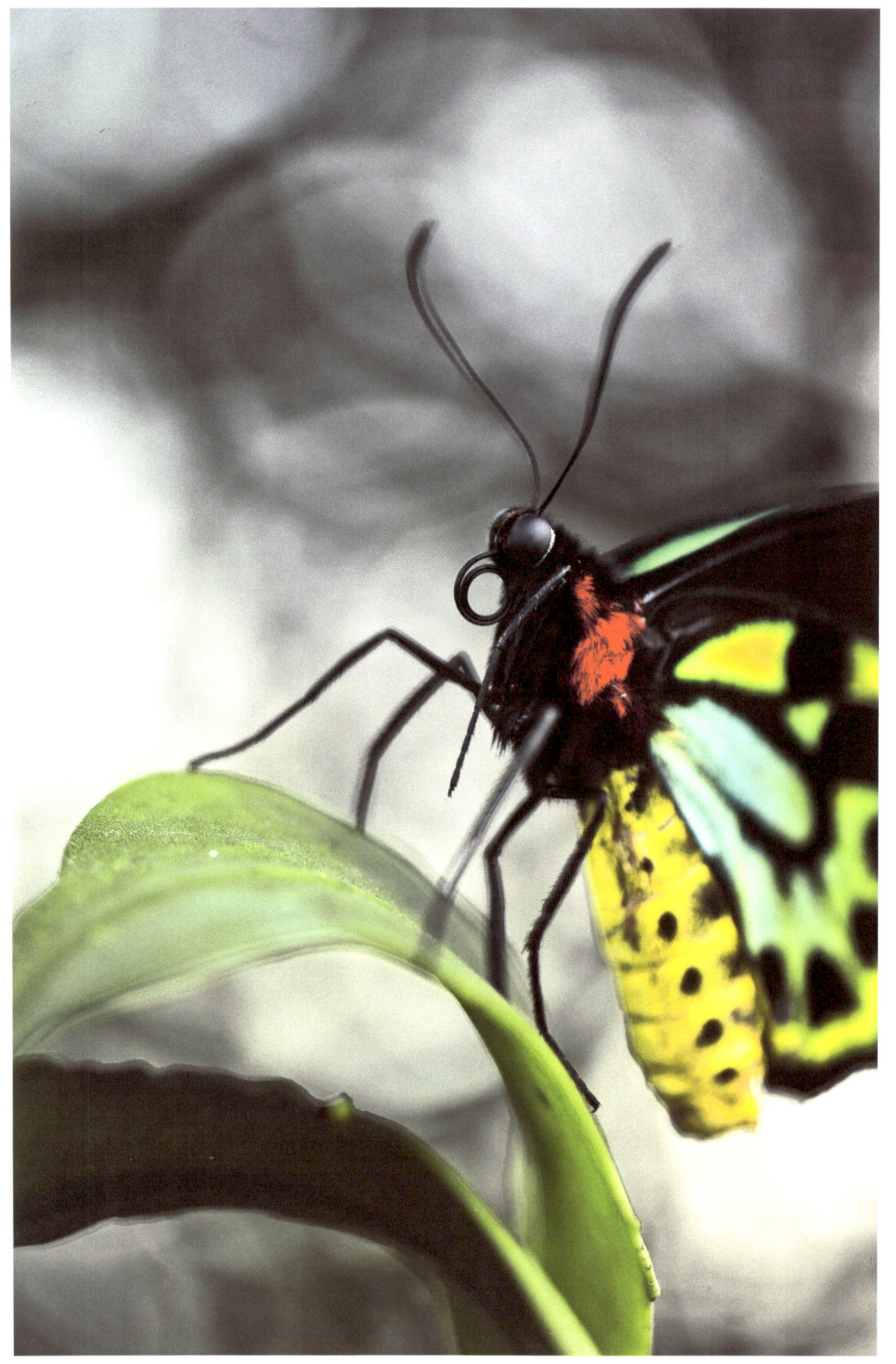

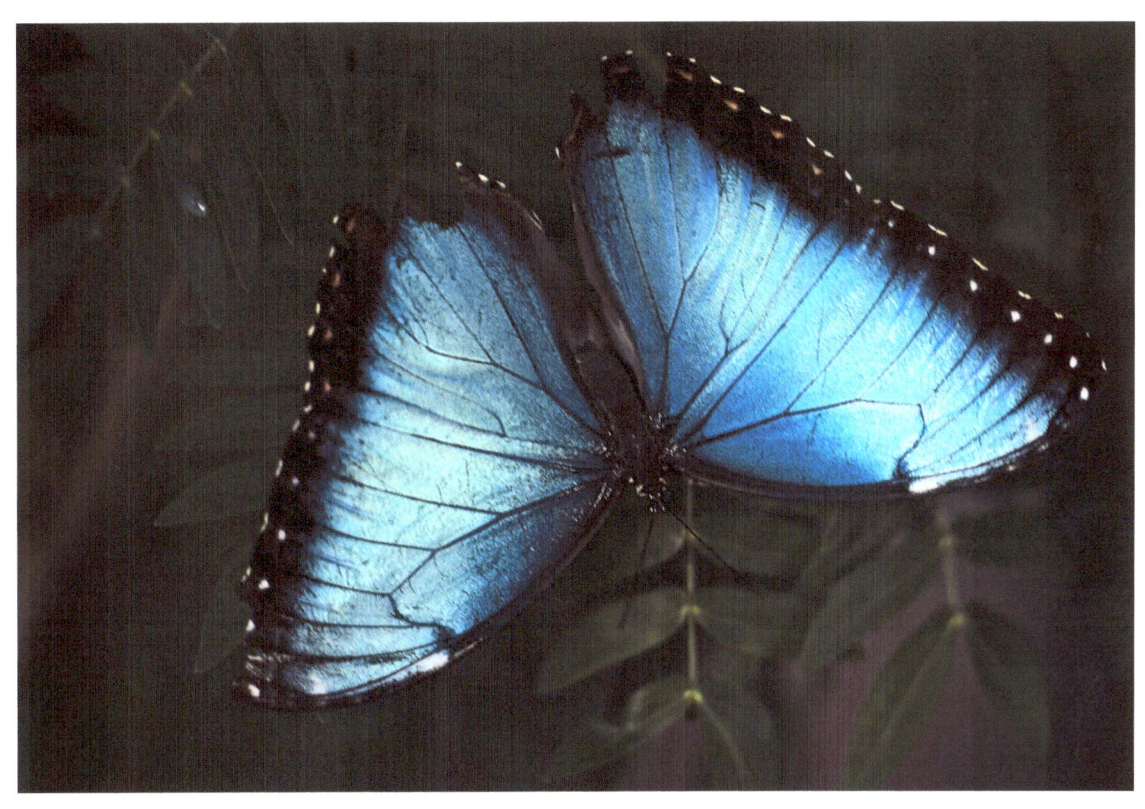

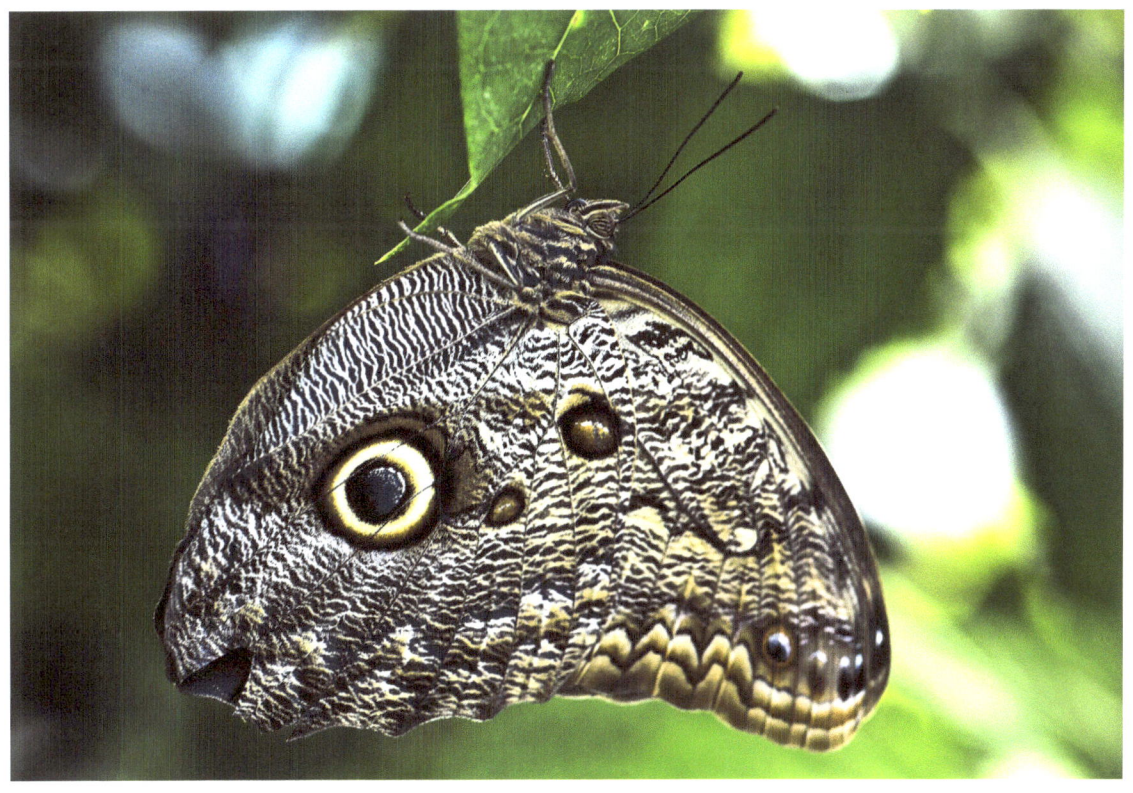

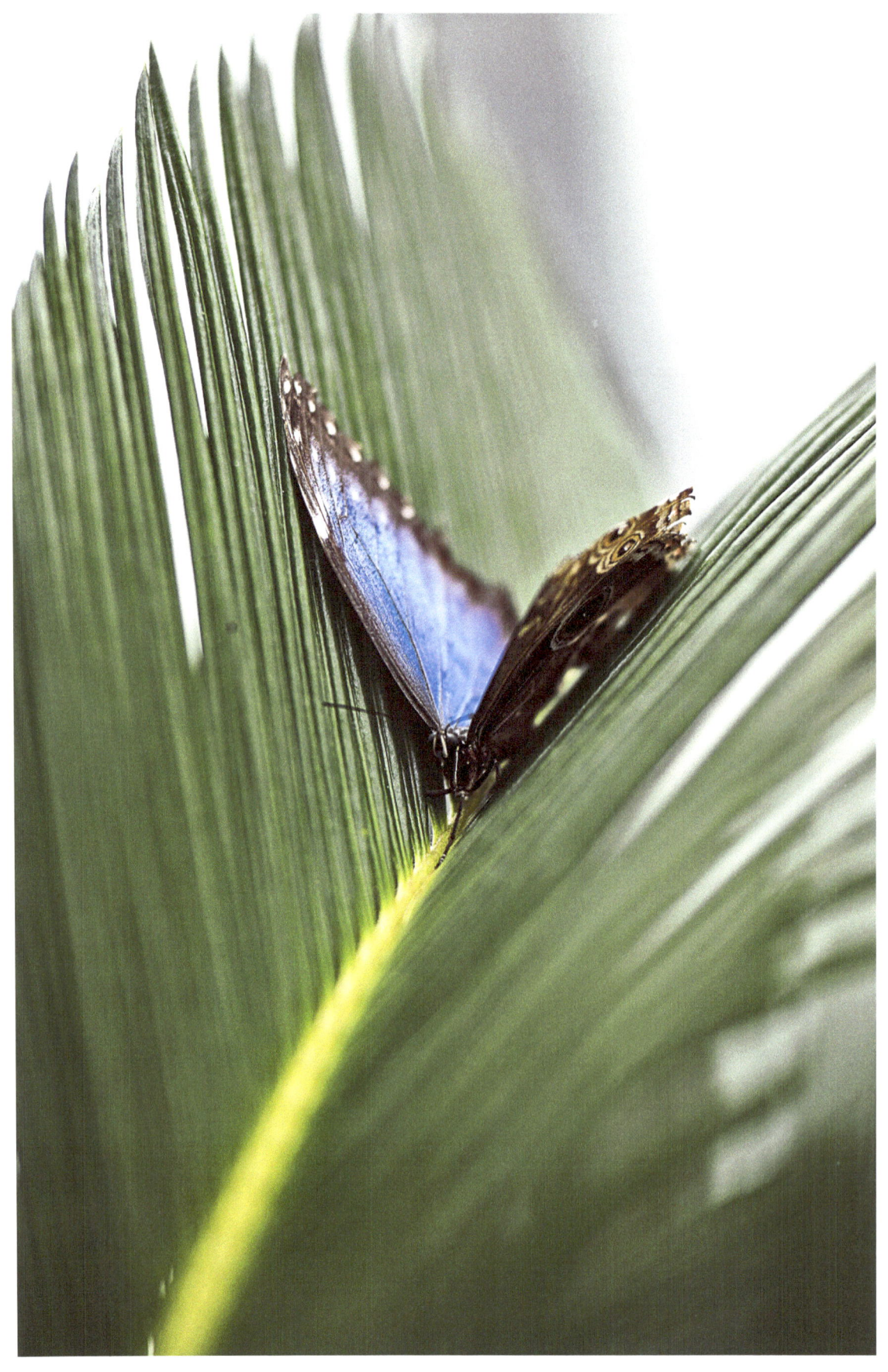

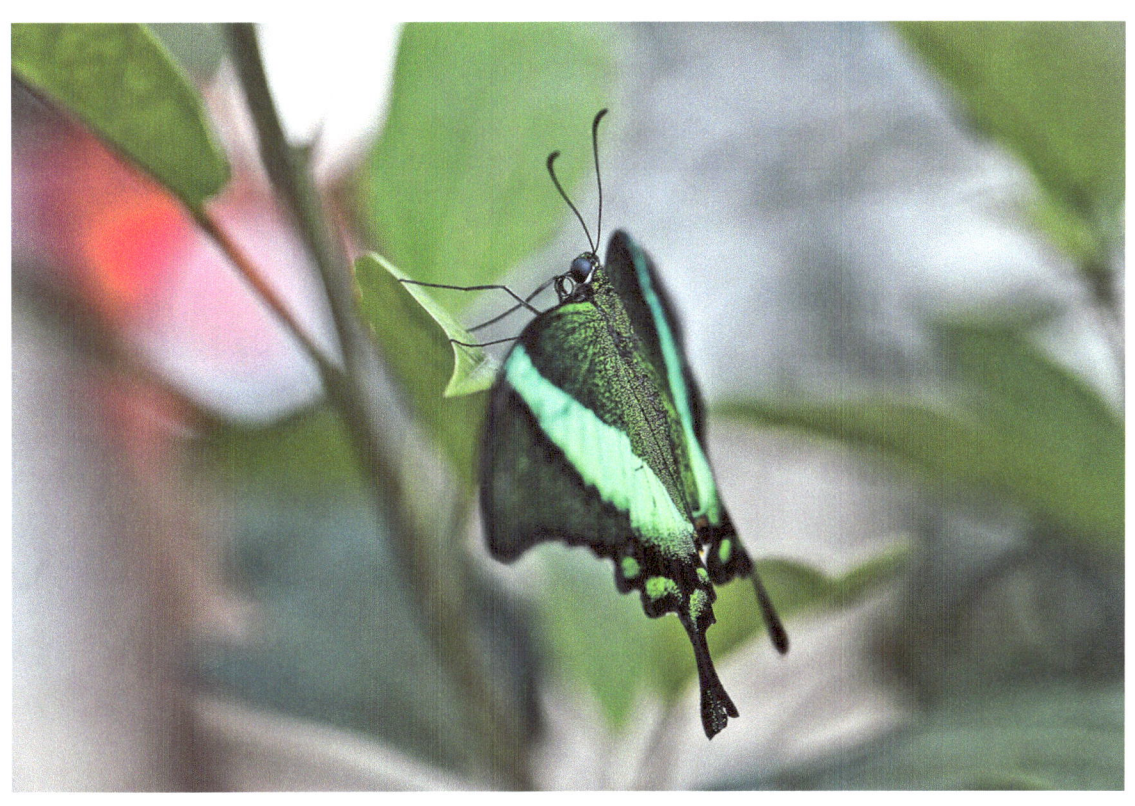

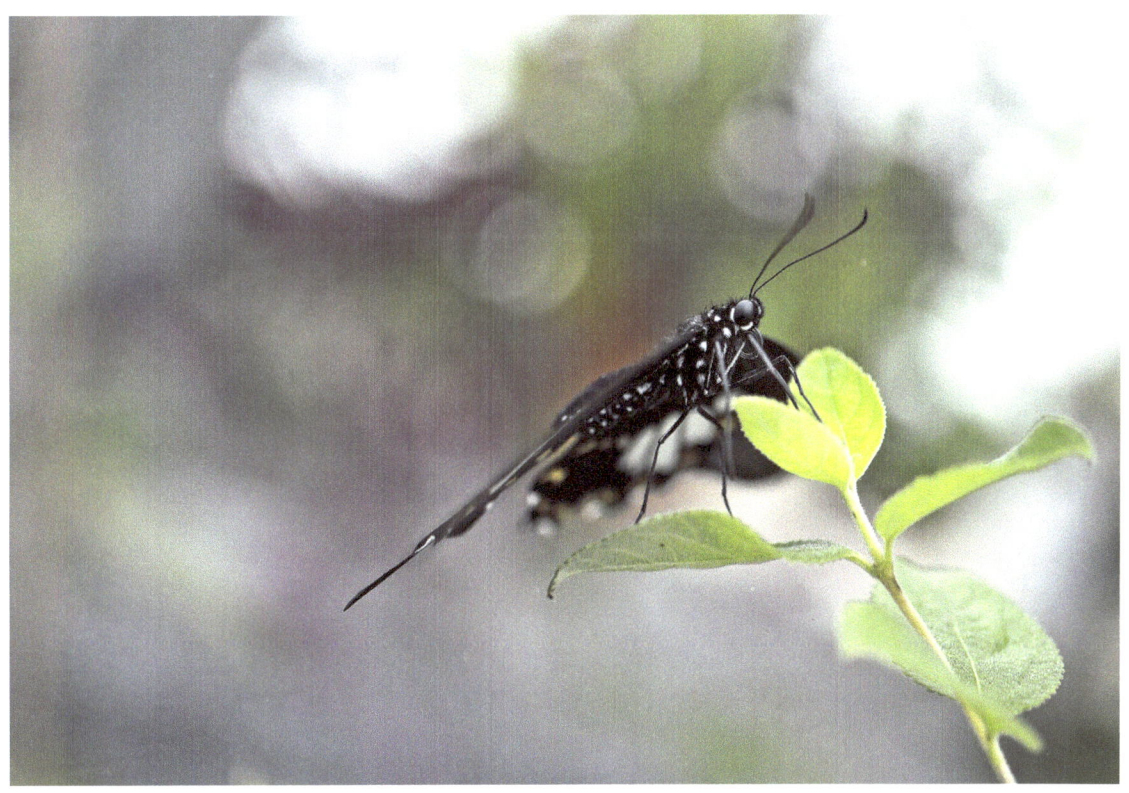

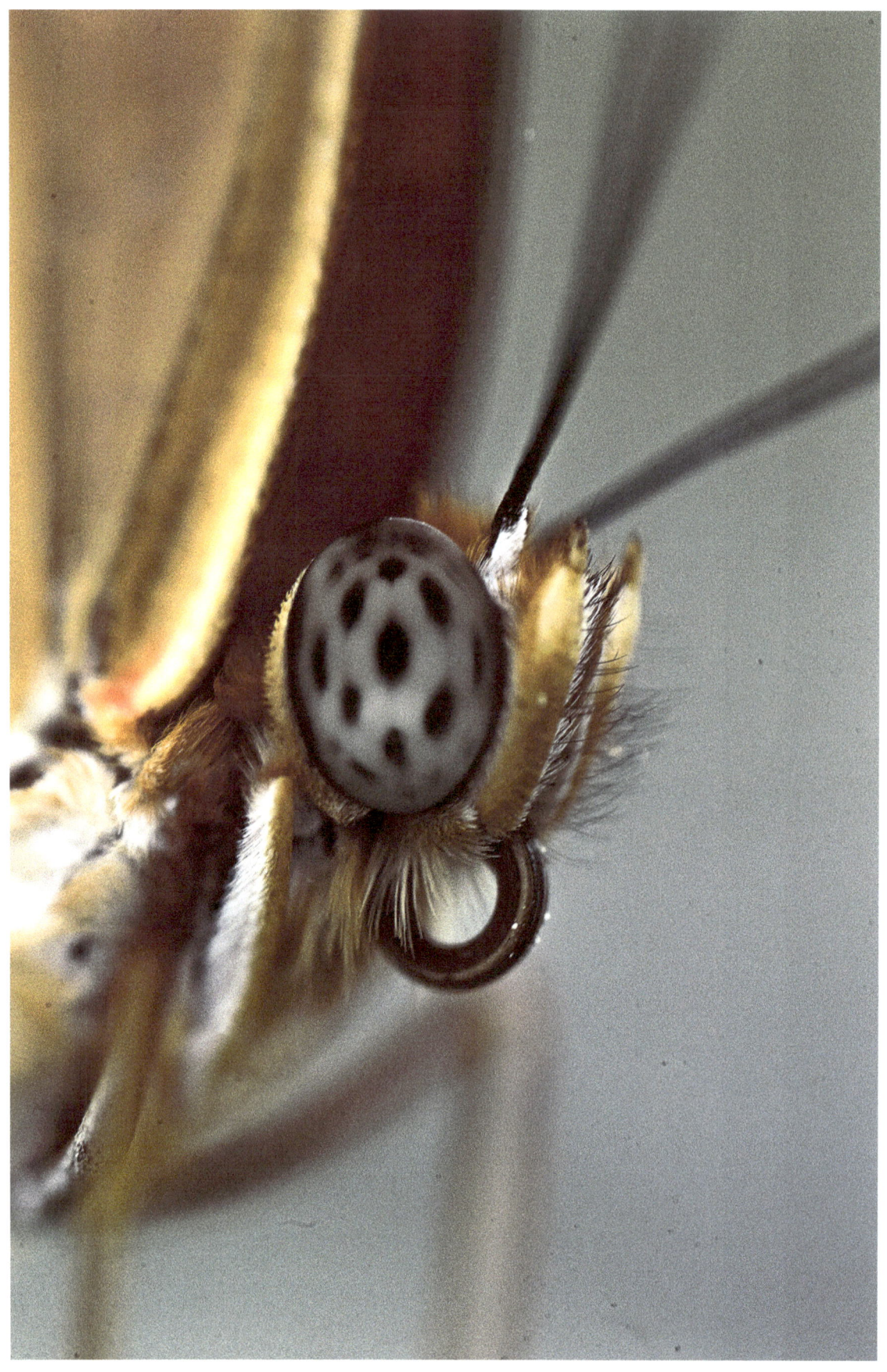

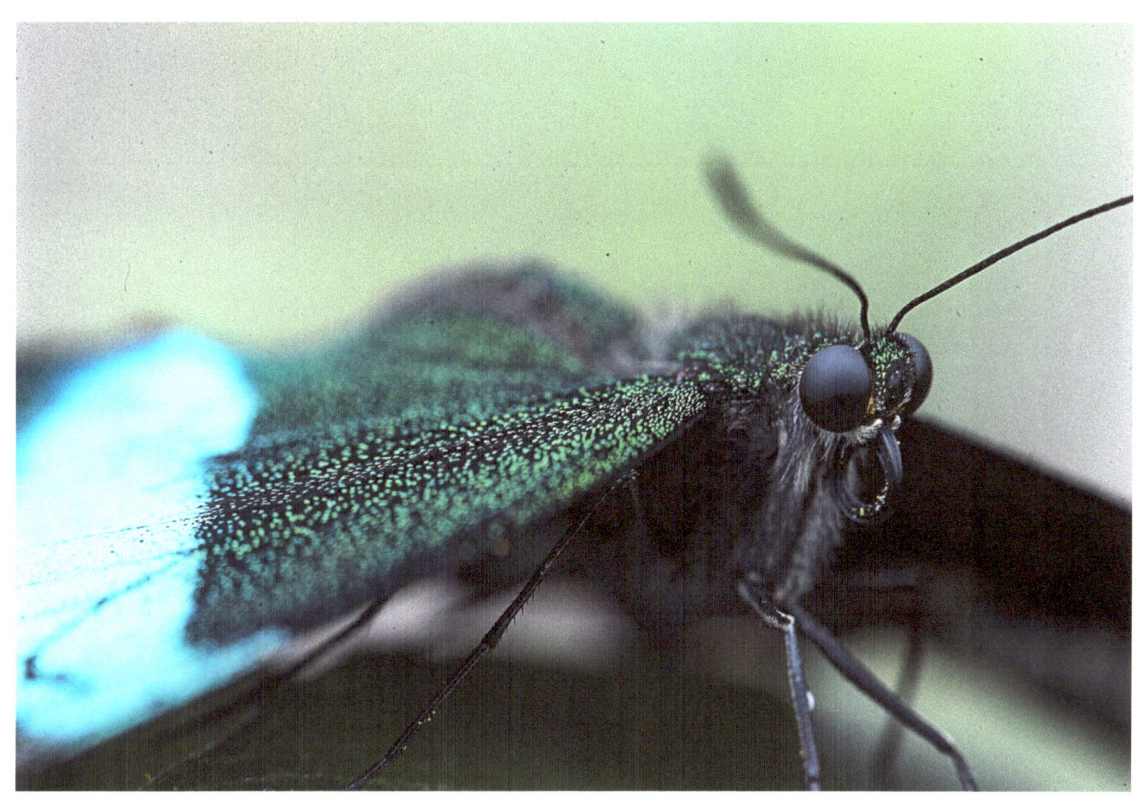

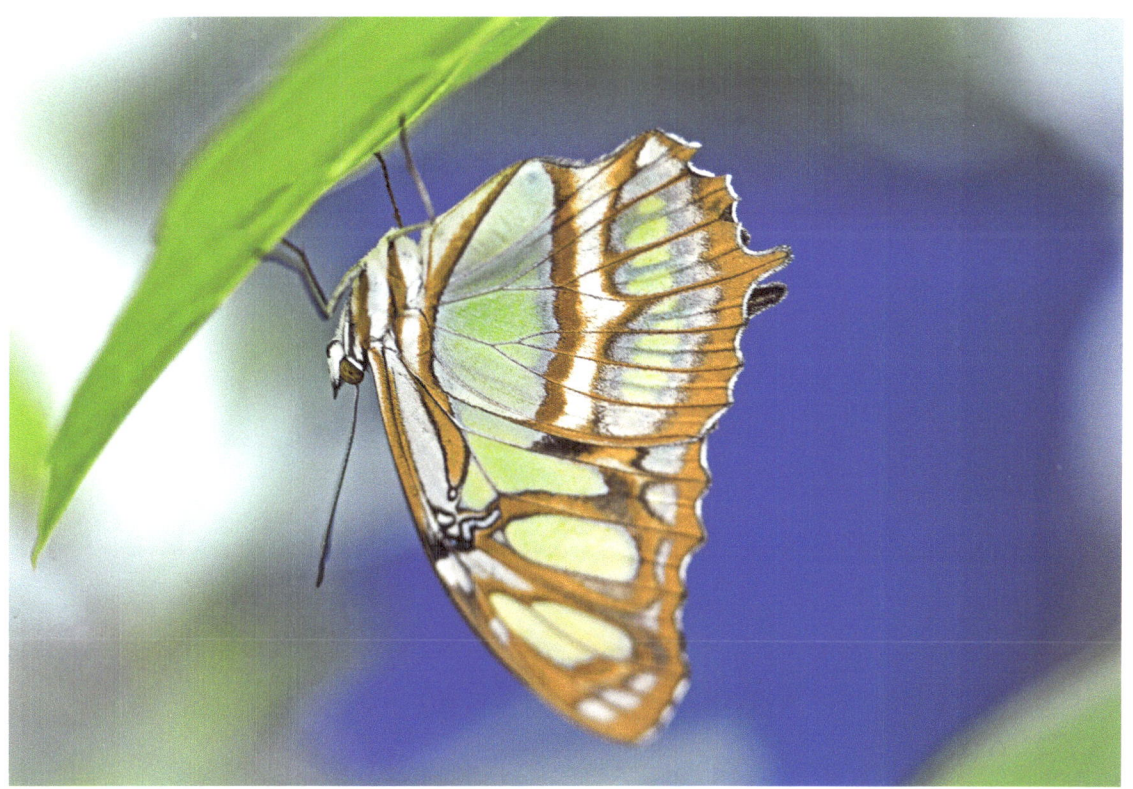

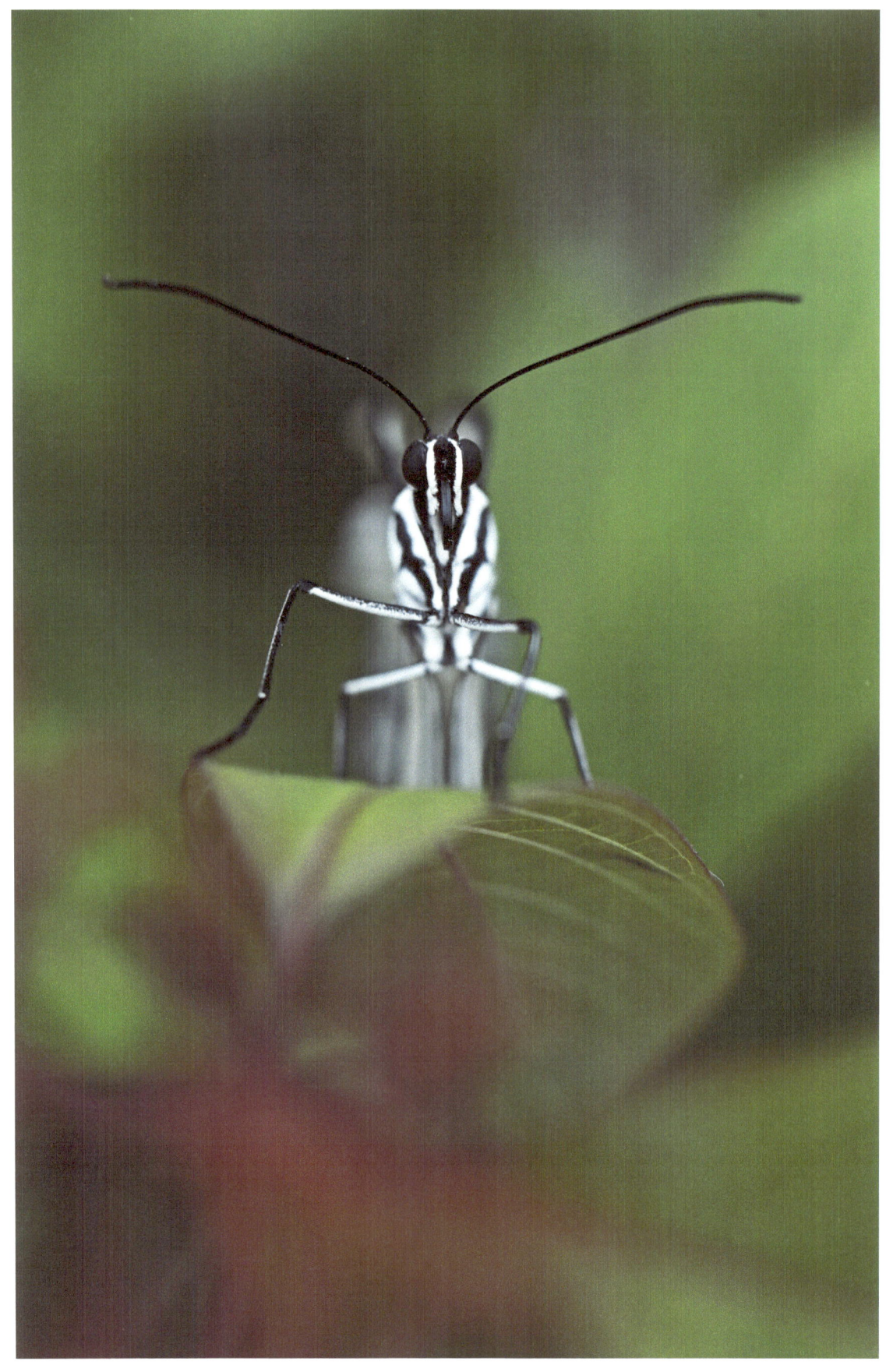

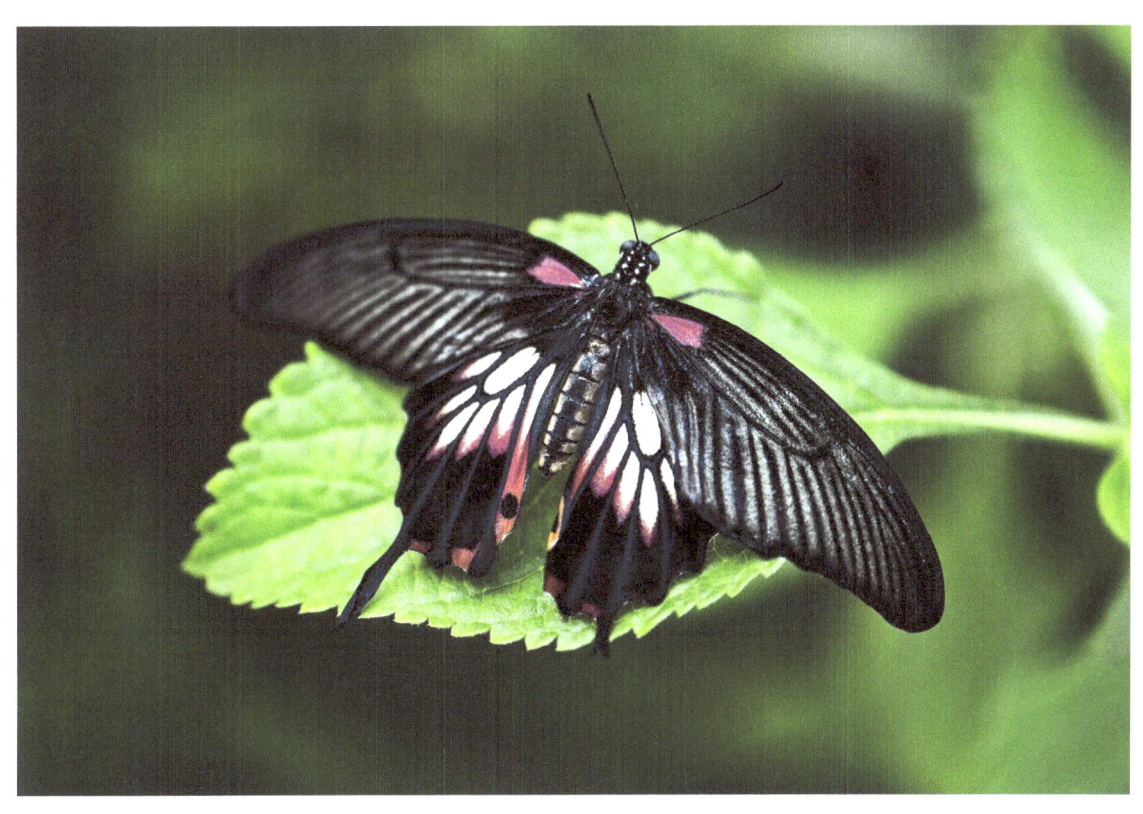

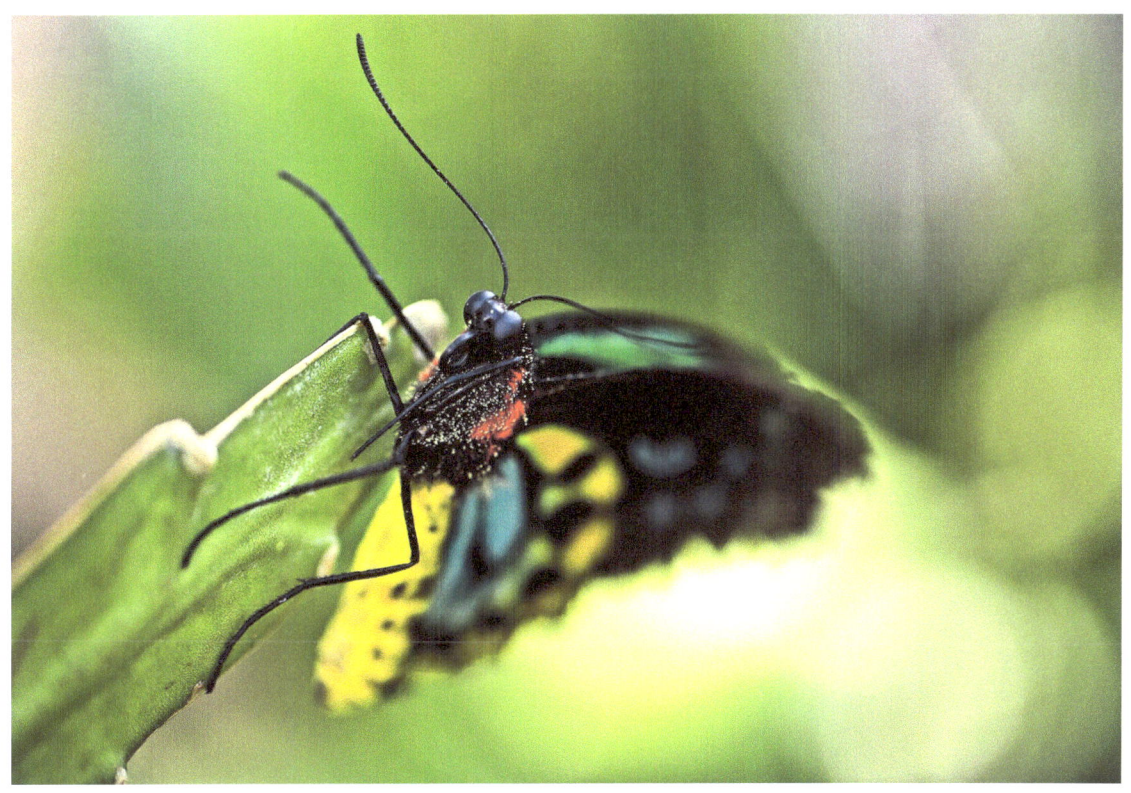

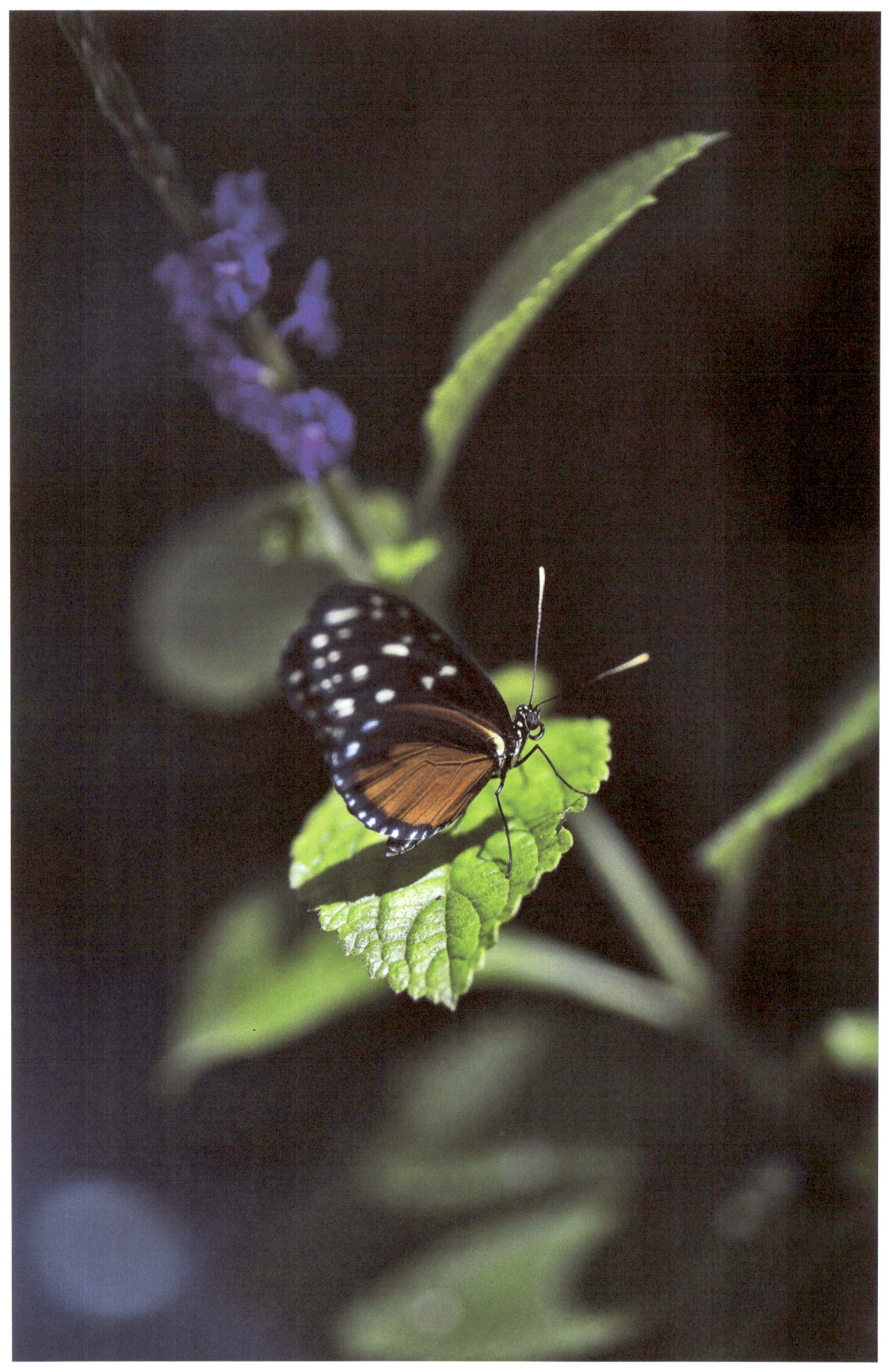

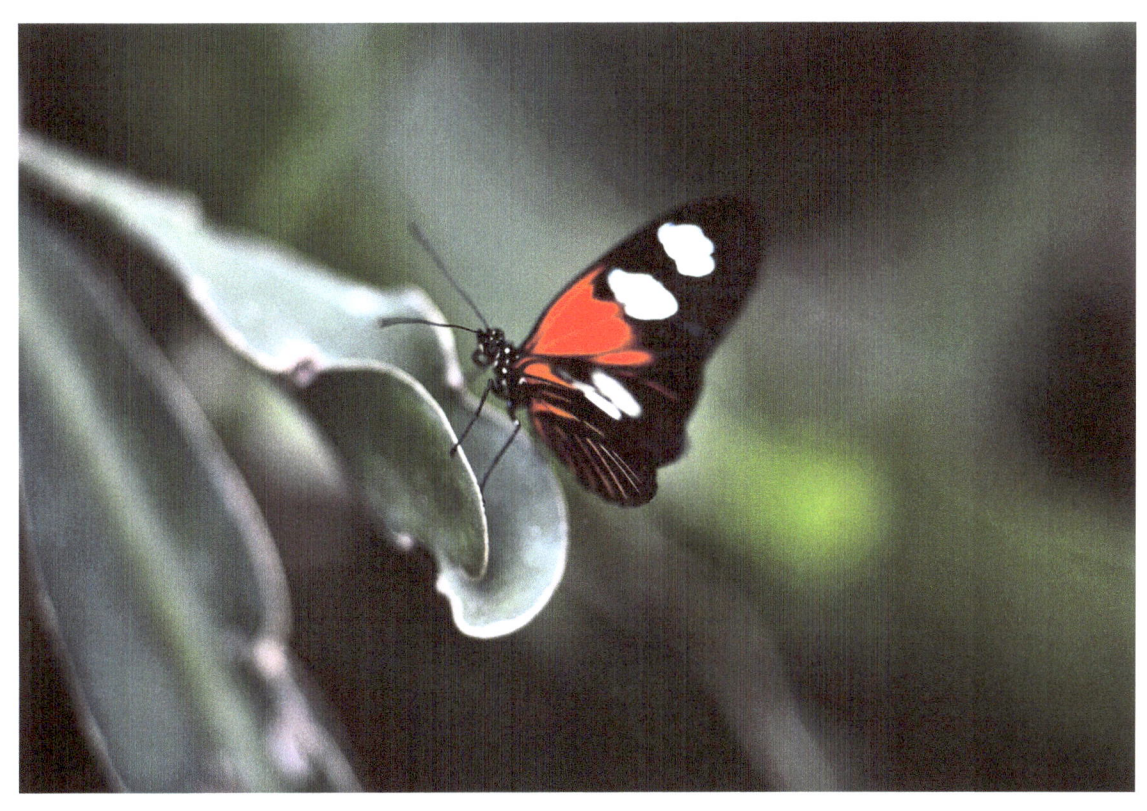

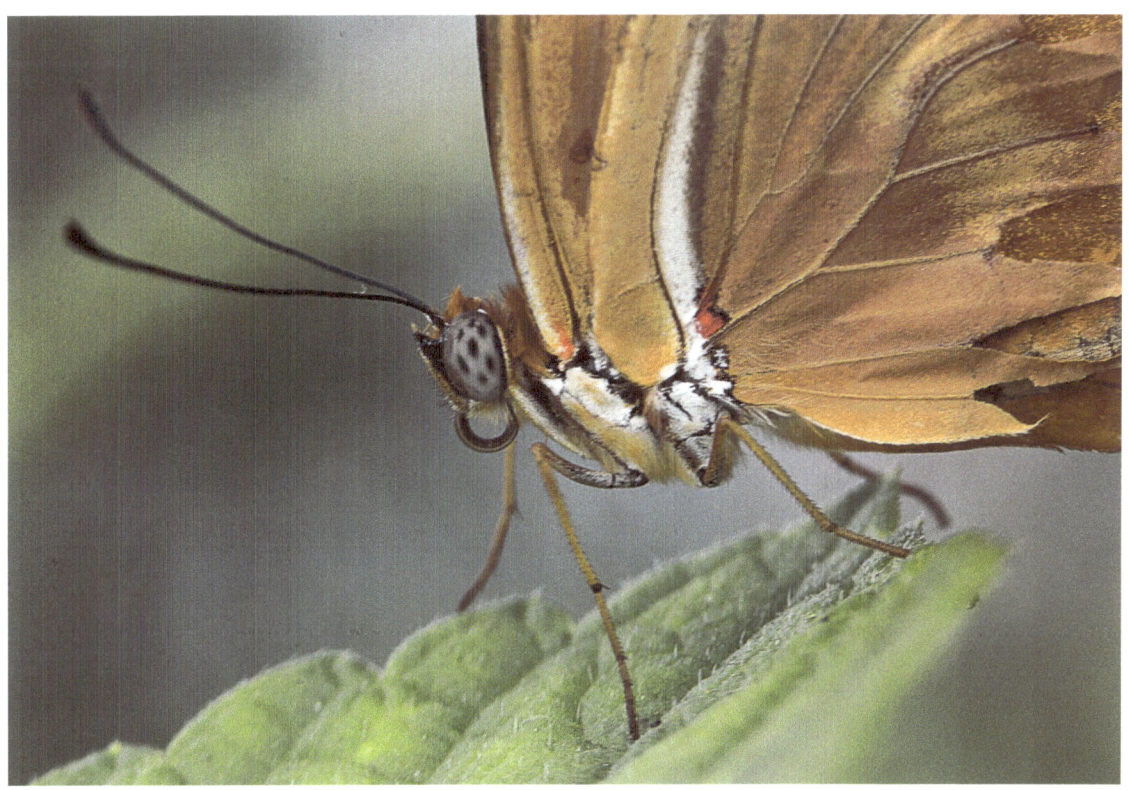

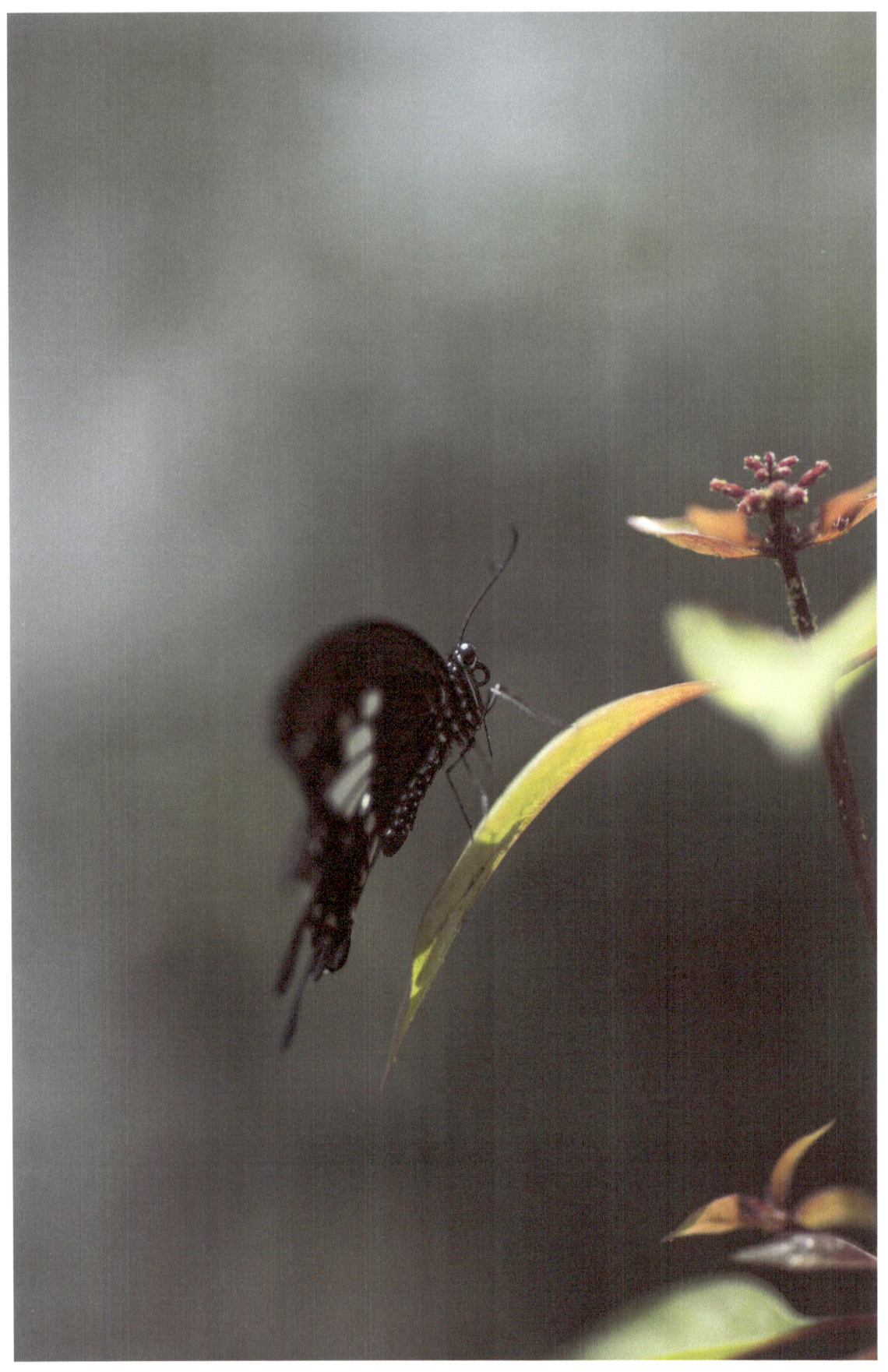

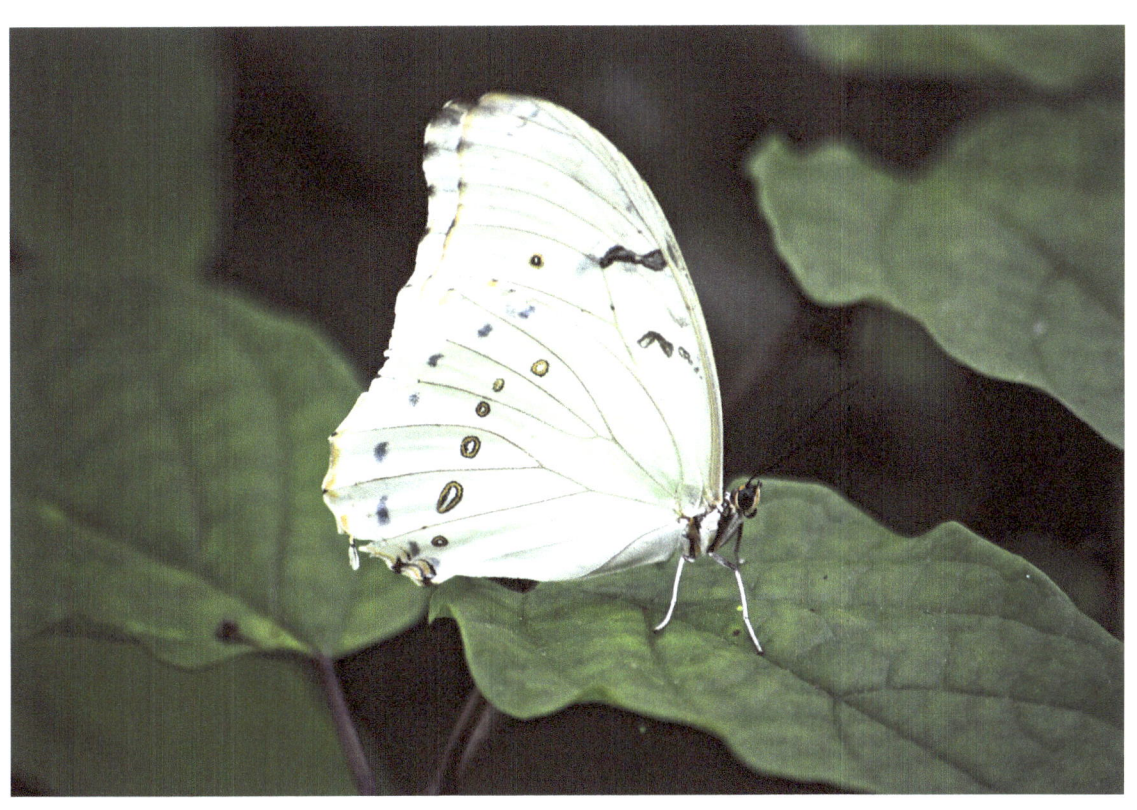

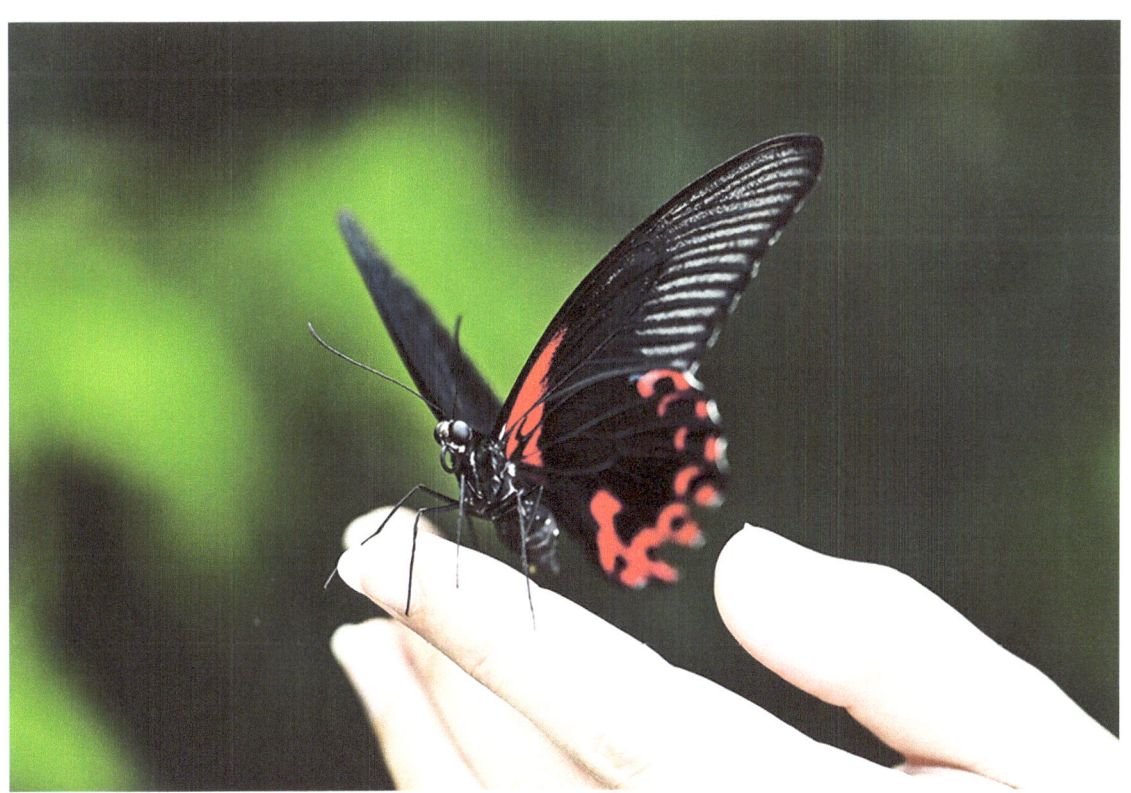

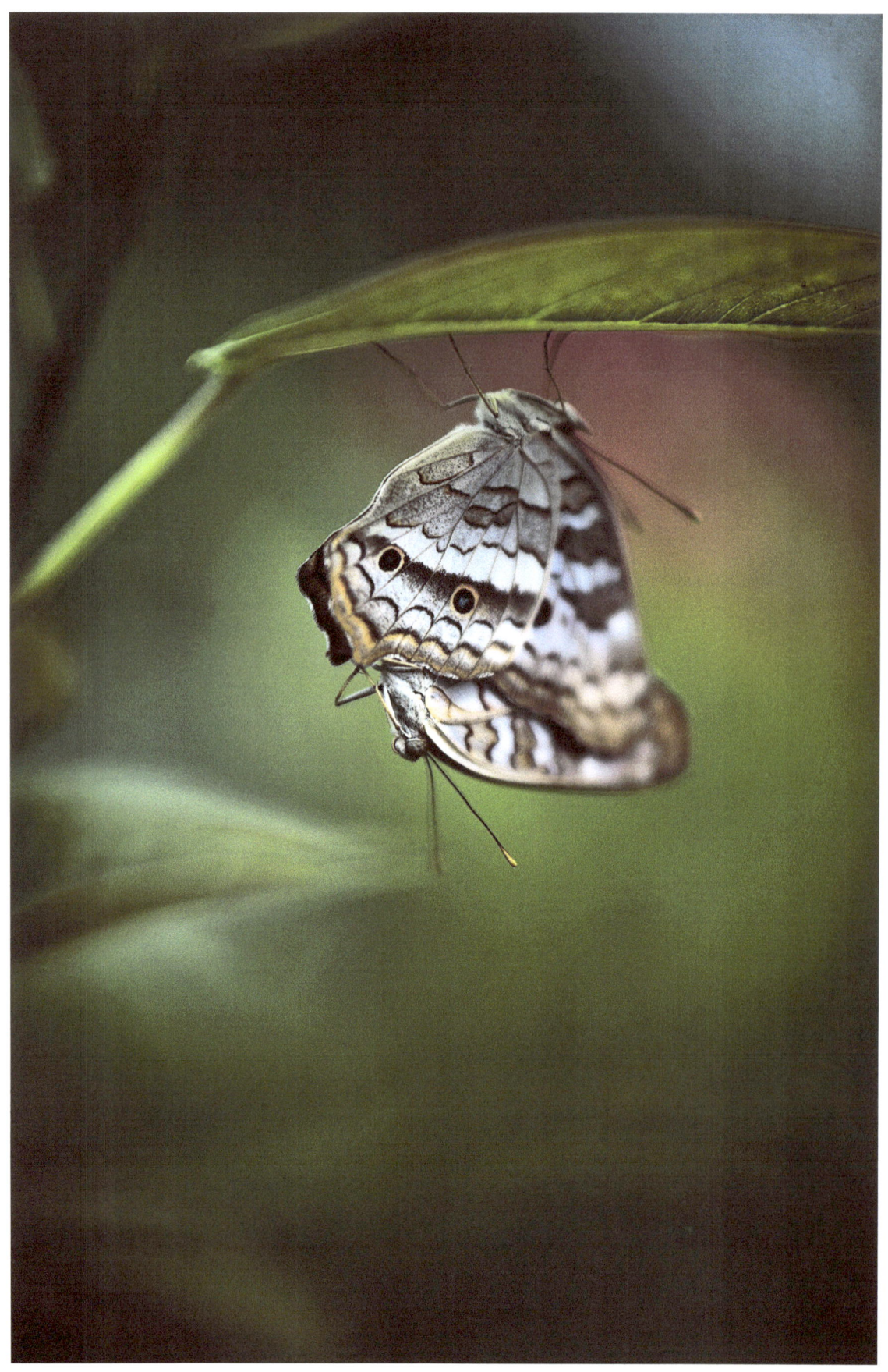

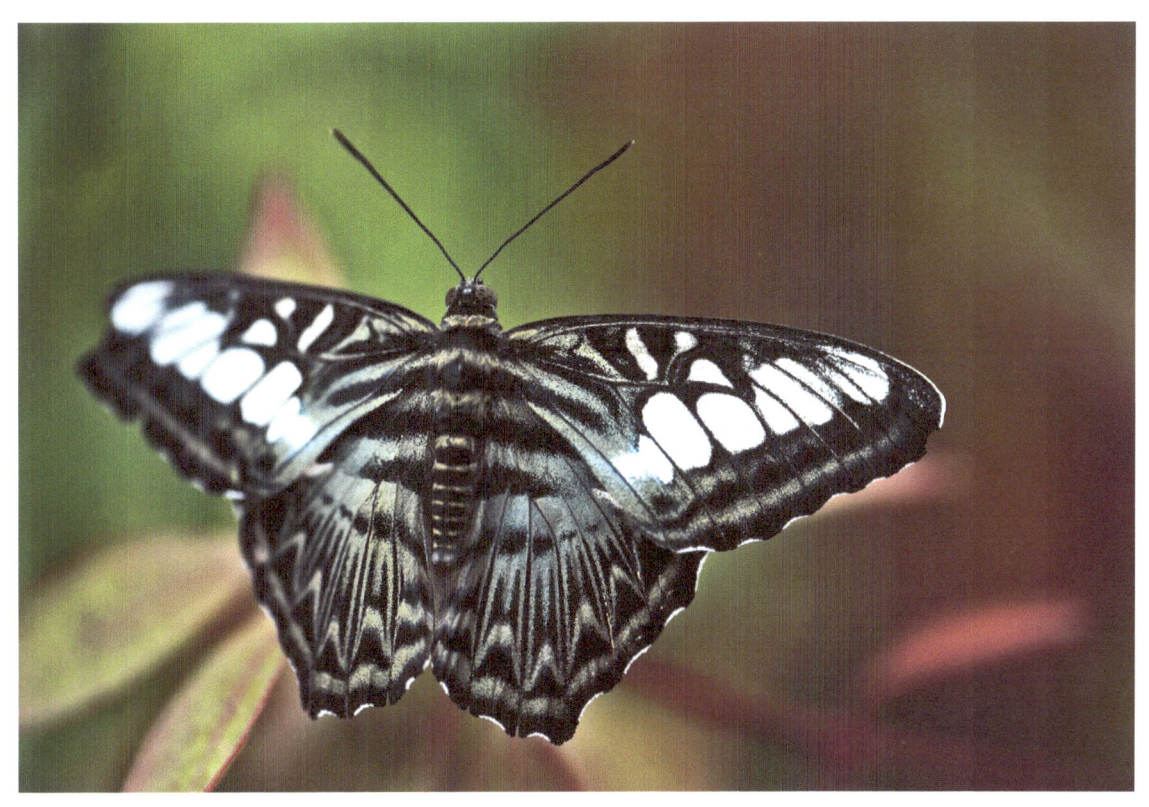

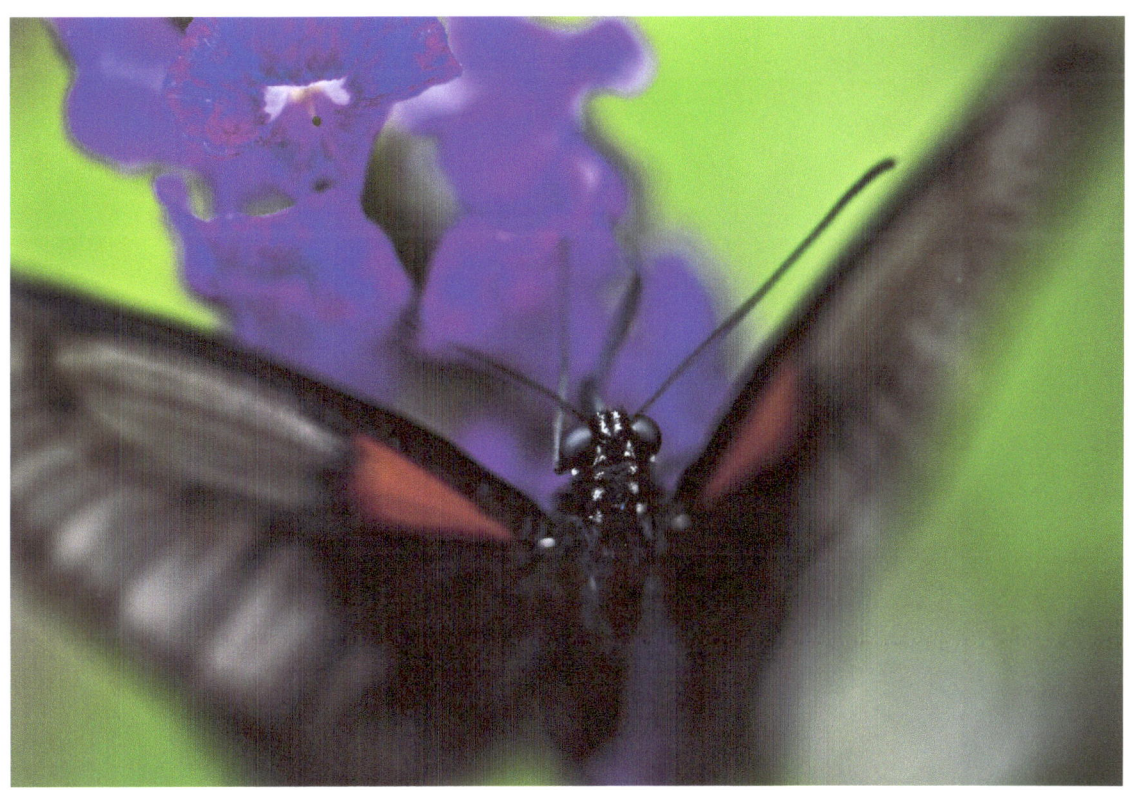

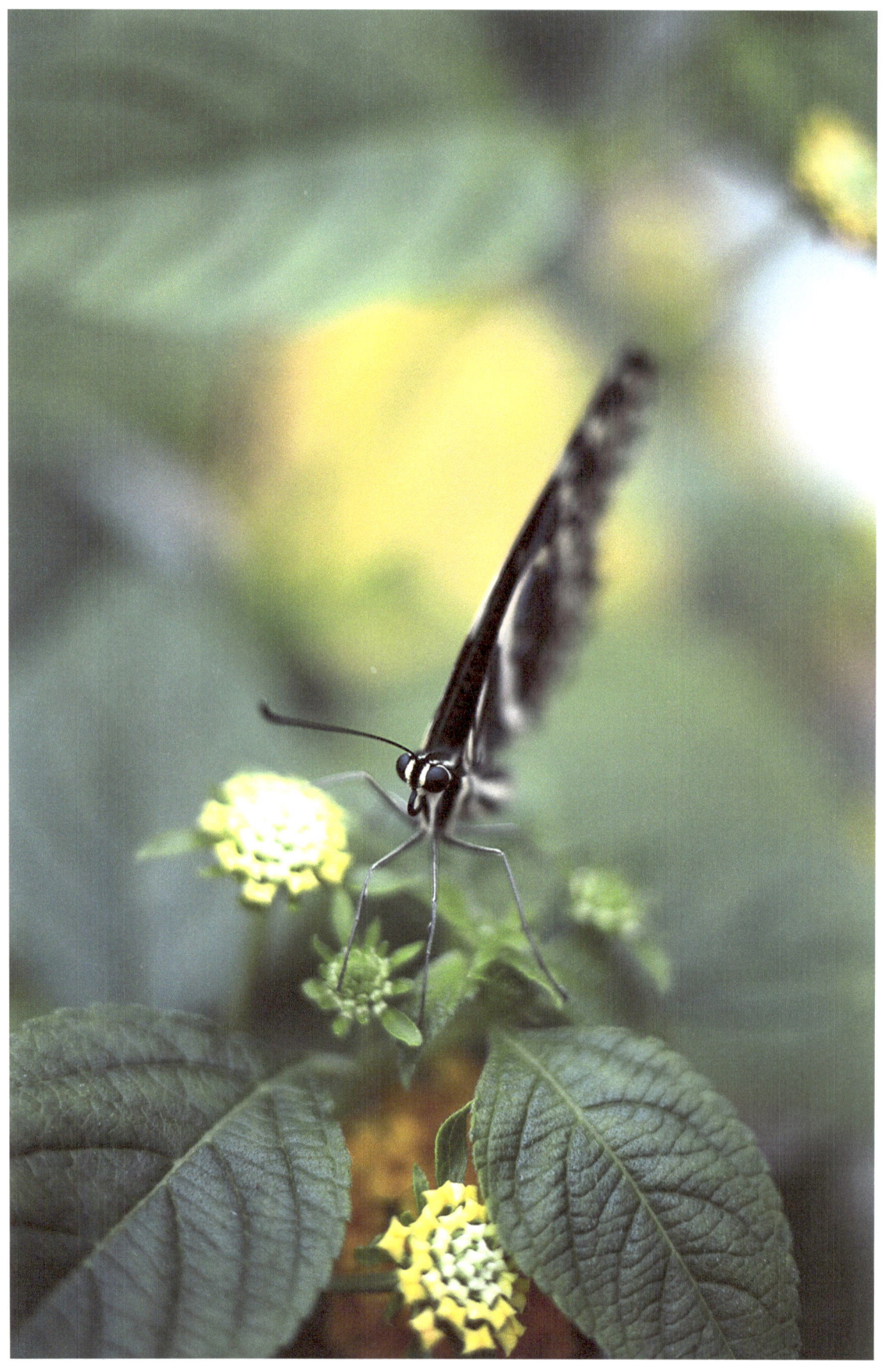

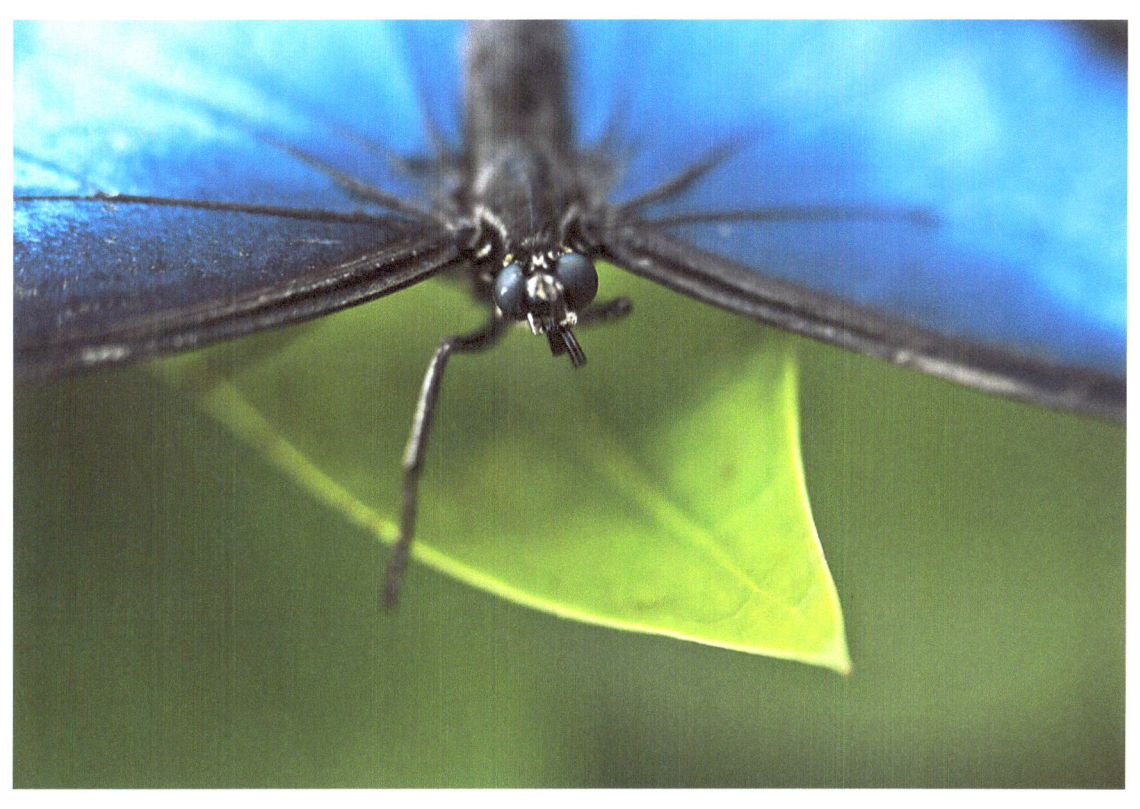

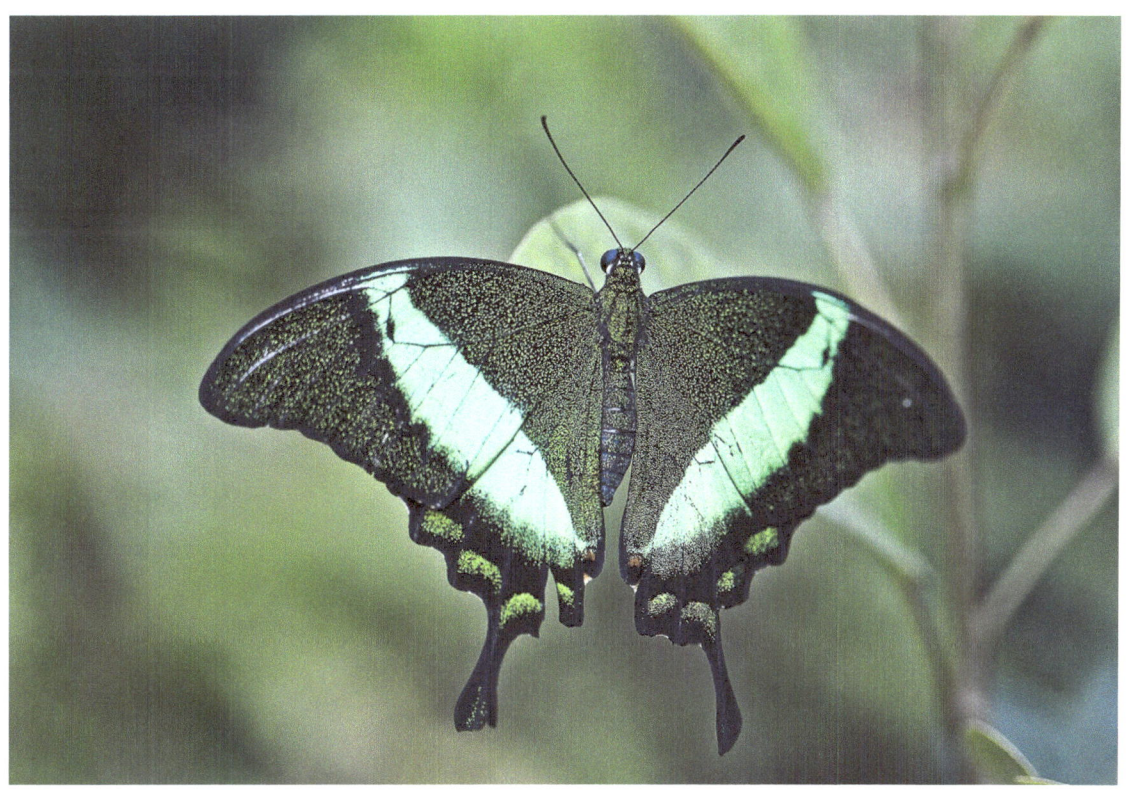

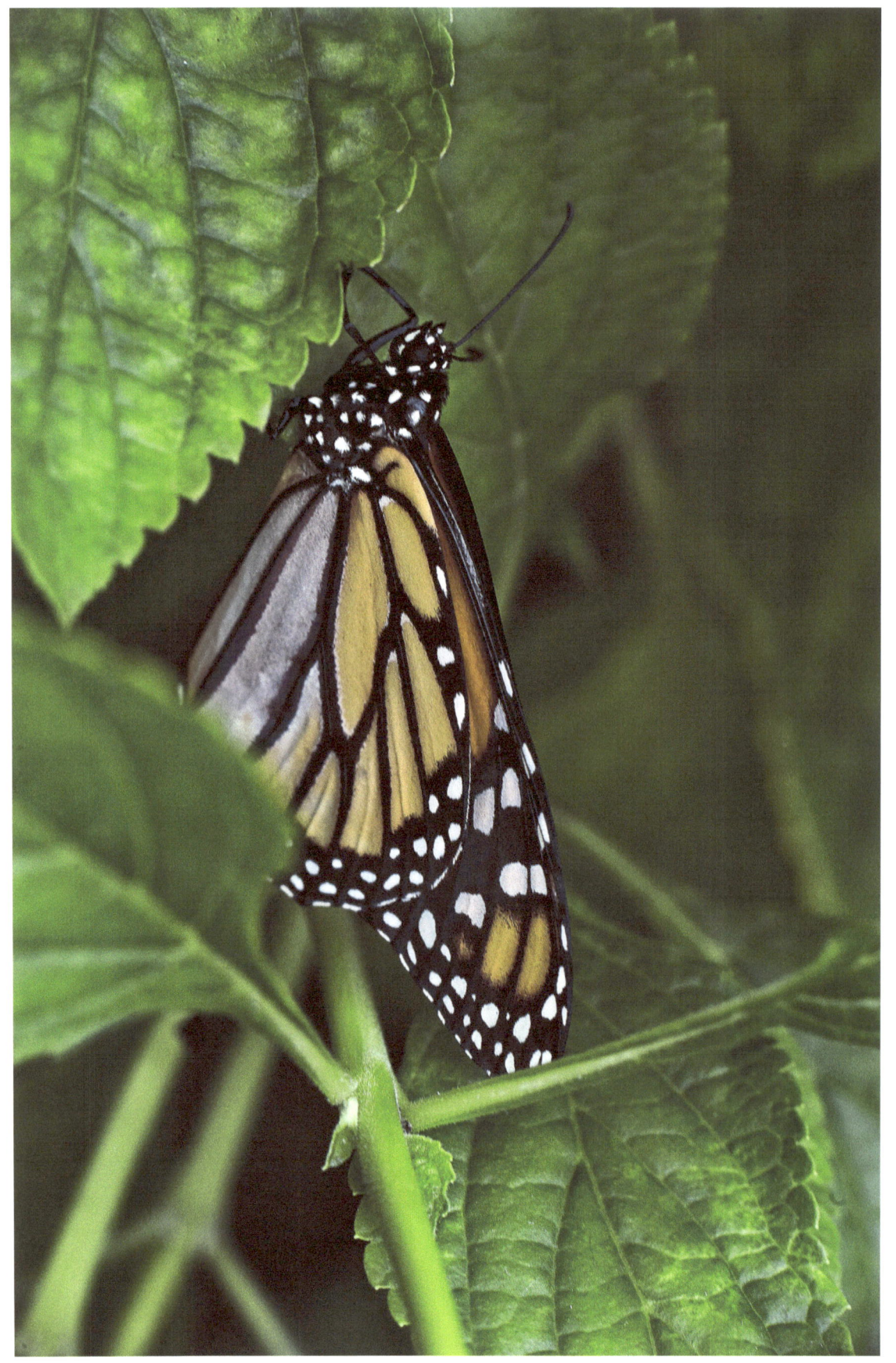

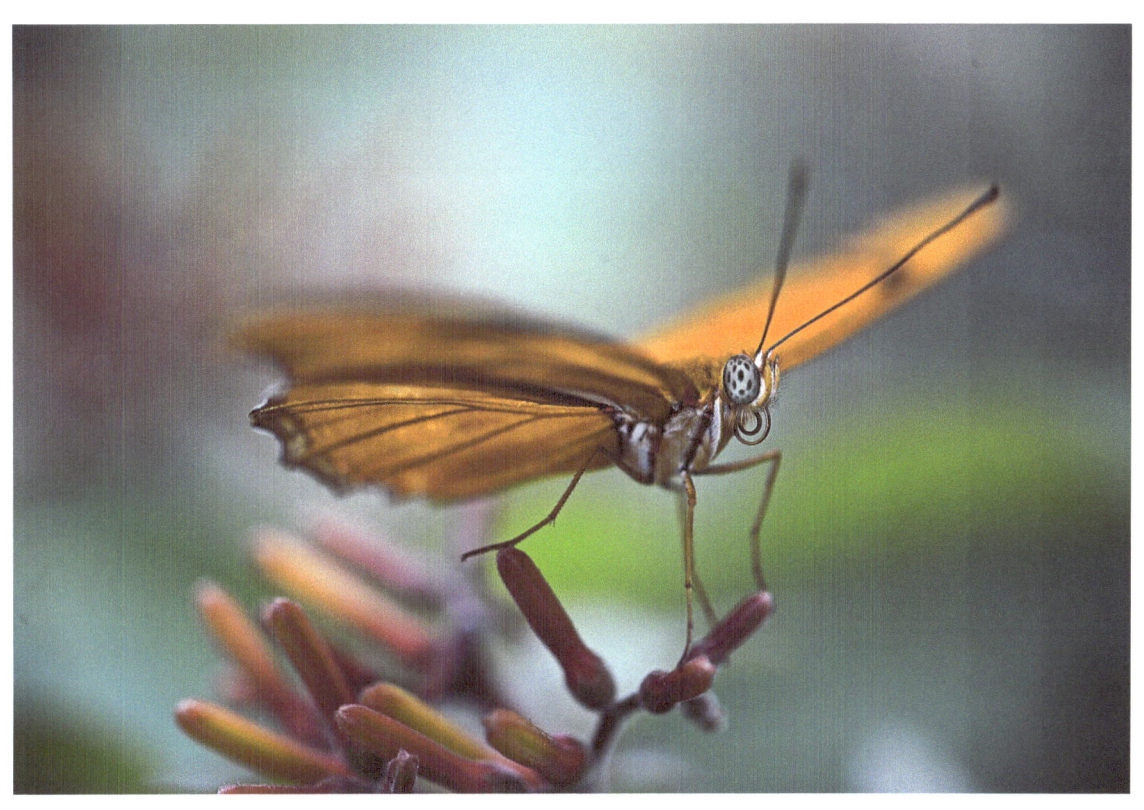

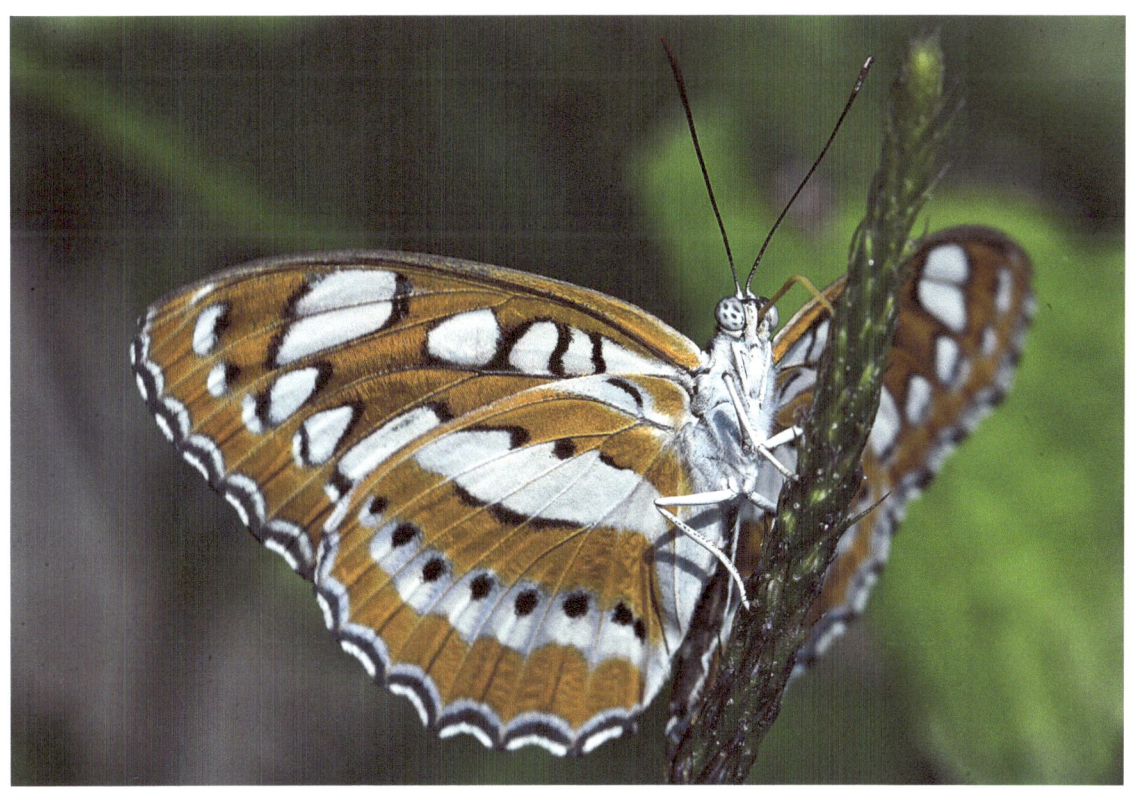

www.ingramcontent.com/pod-product-compliance
Lightning Source LLC
Chambersburg PA
CBHW060835290526
45792CB00006BB/1941